Wedding Band

A Love/Hate Story in
Black and White

by Alice Childress

A SAMUEL FRENCH ACTING EDITION

SAMUEL FRENCH

FOUNDED 1830

New York Hollywood London Toronto

SAMUELFRENCH.COM

WEDDING BAND was first presented by the New York Shakespeare Public Theater, directed by Joseph Papp and Alice Childress on November 26, 1972. The setting was by Ming Cho Lee; costumes by Theoni V. Aldredge; lighting by Martin Aronstein; produced by Joseph Papp, with Bernard Gersten the associate producer. The cast was as follows:

JULIA AUGUSTINE	*Ruby Dee*
TEETA	*Calisse Dinwiddie*
MATTIE	*Juanita Clark*
LULA GREEN	*Hilda Haynes*
FANNY JOHNSON	*Clarice Taylor*
NELSON GREEN	*Albert Hall*
BELL MAN	*Brandon Maggart*
PRINCESS	*Vicky Geyer*
HERMAN	*James Broderick*
ANNABELLE	*Polly Holiday*
HERMAN'S MOTHER	*Jean David*

CHARACTERS
(In Order of Appearance)

JULIA AUGUSTINE

TEETA

MATTIE

LULA GREEN

FANNY JOHNSON

NELSON GREEN

THE BELL MAN

PRINCESS

HERMAN

ANNABELLE

HERMAN'S MOTHER

Wedding Band

ACT ONE

SCENE 1

TIME: *Summer 1918 . . . Saturday morning. A city by the sea . . . South Carolina, U.S.A.*

SCENE: *Three houses in a backyard. The center house is newly painted and cheery looking in contrast to the other two which are weather-beaten and shabby. Center house is gingerbready . . . odds and ends of "picked up" shutters, picket railing, wrought iron railing, newel posts, a Grecian pillar, odd window boxes of flowers . . . everything clashes with a beautiful, subdued splendor; the old and new mingles in defiance of style and period. The playing areas of the houses are raised platforms furnished according to the taste of each tenant. Only one room of each house is visible.* JULIA AUGUSTINE [*tenant of the center house*] *has recently moved in and there is still unpacking to be done. Paths are worn from the houses to the front yard entry. The landlady's house and an outhouse are off-stage. An outdoor hydrant supplies water.*

JULIA *is sleeping on the bed in the center house.* TEETA, *a girl about eight years old, enters the yard from the Stage Right house. She tries to control her weeping as she examines a clump of grass. The muffled weeping disturbs* JULIA'S *sleep. She starts up, half rises from her pillow, then falls back into a troubled sleep.* MATTIE, TEETA'S *mother, enters carrying a switch and fastening her clothing. She joins the little girl in the search for a lost quarter. The search is subdued, intense.*

MATTIE. You better get out there and get it! Did you find it? Gawd, what've I done to be treated this way! You gon' get a whippin' too.

FANNY. (*Enters from the front entry. She is landlady and the self-appointed, fifty-year-old representative of her race.*) Listen, Mattie . . . I want some quiet out here this mornin'.

MATTIE. Dammit, this gal done lost the only quarter I got to my name. (LULA *enters from the direction of the outhouse carrying a covered slop jar. She is forty-five and motherly.*) "Teeta," I say, "Go to the store, buy three cent grits, five cent salt pork, ten cent sugar; and keep your hand closed 'roun' my money." How I'm gonna sell any candy if I got no sugar to make it? You little heifer! (*Goes after* TEETA *who hides behind* LULA.)

LULA. Gawd, help us to find it.

MATTIE. Your daddy is off sailin' the ocean and you got nothin' to do but lose money! *I'm gon' put you out in the damn street, that's what!* (TEETA *cries out.* JULIA *sits up in the bed and cries out.*)

JULIA. No . . . no . . .

FANNY. You disturbin' the only tenant who's paid in advance.

LULA. Teeta, retrace your steps. Show Lula what you did.

TEETA. I hop-hop-hop . . . (*Hops near a post-railing of* JULIA'S *porch.*)

MATTIE. What the hell you do that for?

LULA. There 'tis! That's a quarter . . . down in the hole . . . Can't reach it . . . (JULIA *is now fully awake. Putting on her house-dress over her camisole and petticoat.* MATTIE *takes an axe from the side of the house to knock the post out of the way.*) Aw, *move,* move! That's all the money I got. I'll tear this damn house down and you with it!

FANNY. And I'll blow this police whistle. (JULIA *steps out on the porch. She is an attractive brown woman about thirty-five years old.*)

MATTIE. Blow it . . . blow it . . . blow it . . . hot damn— (*Near tears. She decides to tell* JULIA *off also.*) I'll tear it down—that's right. If you don't like it—come on down here and whip me.

JULIA. (*Nervous but determined to present a firm stand.*) Oh, my . . . Good mornin' ladies. My name is Julia Augustine. I'm not gonna move.

LULA. My name is Lula. Why you think we wantcha to move?

FANNY. Miss Julia, I'm sorry your first day starts like this. Some people are ice cream and others just cow-dung. I try to be ice cream.

MATTIE. Dammit, I'm ice cream too. Strawberry. (*Breaks down and cries.*)

FANNY. That's Mattie. She lost her last quarter, gon' break down my house to get it.

JULIA. (*Gets a quarter from her dresser.*) Oh my, dear heart, don't cry. Take this twenty-five cents, Miss Mattie.

MATTIE. No thank you, ma'm.

JULIA. And I have yours under my house for good luck.

FANNY. Show your manners.

TEETA. Thank you. You the kin'est person in the worl'. (LULA *enters her house.* TEETA *starts for home, then turns to see if her mother is coming.*)

MATTIE. (*To* JULIA.) I didn't mean no harm. But my husband October's in the Merchant Marine and I needs my little money. Well, thank you. (*To* TEETA.) Come on, honey bunch. (*She enters her house Stage Right.* TEETA *proudly follows.* LULA *is putting* NELSON's *breakfast on the table at Stage Left.*)

FANNY. (*Testing strength of post.*) My poor father's turnin' in his grave. He built these rent houses just 'fore he died . . . And he wasn't a carpenter. Shows what the race can do when we wanta. (*Feels the porch railing and tests its strength.*) That loud-mouth Mattie used to work in a white cat-house.

JULIA. A what?

FANNY. Sportin' house, house of . . . A whore house. know what she used to do?

JULIA. (*Embarrassed.*) Not but so many things *to* do, I guess. (FANNY *wants to follow her in the house but* JULIA *fends her off.*)

FANNY. Used to wash their joy-towels. Washin' joy-towels for one cent apiece. I wouldn't work in that kinda place—would you?

JULIA. Indeed not.

FANNY. Vulgarity.

JULIA. (*Trying to get away.*) I have my sewing to do now, Miss Fanny.

FANNY. I got a lovely piece-a blue serge. Six yards. (*She attempts to get into the house but* JULIA *deftly blocks the door.*)

JULIA. I don't sew for people. (FANNY *wonders why not.*) I do homework for a store . . . hand-finishin' on ladies' shirtwaists.

FANNY. You 'bout my age . . . I'm thirty-five.

JULIA. (*After a pause.*) I thought you were younger.

FANNY. (*Genuinely moved by the compliment.*) Thank you. But I'm not married 'cause nobody's come up to my high standard. Where you get them expensive-lookin', high-class shoes?

JULIA. In a store. I'm busy now, Miss Fanny.

FANNY. Doin' what?

JULIA. First one thing then another. Good-day. (*Thinks she has dismissed her. Goes in the house.* FANNY *quickly follows into the room . . . picks up a teacup from the table.*)

FANNY. There's a devil in your tea-cup . . . also prosperity. Tell me 'bout yourself, don't be so distant.

JULIA. It's all there in the tea-leaves.

FANNY. Oh, go on! I'll tell you somethin' . . . that sweet-face Lula killed her only child.

JULIA. No, she didn't.

FANNY. In a way-a speakin'. And then Gawd snatched up her triflin' husband. One nothin' piece-a man. Biggest thing he ever done for her was to lay down and die. Poor woman. Yes indeed, then she went and adopted this fella from the colored orphan home. Boy grew too big for a lone woman to keep in the house. He's a big, strappin', over-grown man now. I wouldn't feel safe livin' with a man that's not blood kin, 'doption or no 'doption. It's 'gainst nature. Oughta see the muscles on him.

JULIA. (Wearily.) Oh, my . . . I think I hear somebody callin' you.

FANNY. Yesterday the white-folks threw a pail-a dirty water on him. A black man on leave got no right to wear his uniform in public. The crackers don't like it. That's flauntin' yourself.

JULIA. Miss Fanny, I don't talk about people.

FANNY. Me neither. (Giving her serious advice.) We high-class, quality people oughta stick together.

JULIA. I really do stay busy.

FANNY. Doin' what? Seein' your beau? You have a beau haven't-cha?

JULIA. (Realizing she must tell her something in order to get rid of her.) Miss Johnson . . .

FANNY. Fanny.

JULIA. (Managing to block her toward the door.) My mother and father have long gone on to Glory.

FANNY. Gawd rest the dead and bless the orphan.

JULIA. Yes, I do have a beau . . . But I'm not much of a mixer. (She now has FANNY out on the porch.)

FANNY. Get time, come up front and see my parlor. I got a horsehair settee and a four piece, silver-plated tea service.

JULIA. Think of that.

FANNY. The first and only one to be owned by a colored

woman in the United States of America. Salesman told me.

JULIA. Oh, just imagine. (MATTIE *enters wearing a blue calico dress and striped apron.*)

FANNY. My mother was a genuine, full-blooded, qualified, Seminole Indian.

TEETA. (*Calls to her mother from the doorway.*) Please . . . Mama . . . Mama . . . Buy me a hair ribbon.

MATTIE. All right! I'm gon' buy my daughter a hair-ribbon.

FANNY. Her hair is so short you'll have to nail it on. (FANNY *exits to her house.*)

MATTIE. That's all right about that, Fanny. Your father worked in a stinkin' phosphate mill . . . yeah, and didn't have a tooth in his head. Then he went and married some half Portuguese woman. I don't call that bein' in no damn society. I works for my livin'. I makes candy and I takes care of a little white girl. Hold this nickel 'til I get back. Case of emergency I don't like Teeta to be broke.

JULIA. I'll be busy today, lady.

MATTIE. (*As she exits carrying a tray of candy.*) Thank you, darlin'.

TEETA. Hey lady, my daddy helps cook food on a big war boat. He peels potatoes. You got any children?

JULIA. No . . . Grace-a Gawd. (*Starts to go in house.*)

TEETA. Hey, lady! Didja ever hear of Philadelphia? After the war that's where we're goin' to live. Philadelphia!

JULIA. Sounds like heaven.

TEETA. Jesus is the President of Philadelphia. (TEETA *sweeps in front of* JULIA's *house. Lights come up in* LULA's *house.* NELSON *is eating breakfast. He is a rather rough-looking muscly fellow with a soft voice and a bittersweet sense of humor. He is dressed in civilian finery and his striped silk shirt seems out of place in the drab little room.* LULA *makes paper flowers, and the colorful bits of paper are seen everywhere as finished and partially finished flowers and stems, also a finished funeral piece. A picture of Abraham Lincoln hangs on the upstage wall.* LULA *is brushing* NELSON'S *uniform jacket.*)

LULA. Last week the Bell Man came to collect the credit payment he says . . . "Auntie, whatcha doin' with Abraham Lincoln's pitcher on the wall? He was such a poor president."

NELSON. Tell the cracker to mind his damn business.

LULA. It don't pay to get mad. Remember yesterday.

NELSON. (*Studying her face for answers.*) Mama, you supposed to get mad when somebody throw a pail-a water on you.

LULA. It's their country and their uniform, so just stay out the way.

NELSON. Right. I'm not goin' back to work in that coal-yard when I get out the army.

LULA. They want you back. A bird in the hand, y'know.

NELSON. A bird in the hand ain't always worth two in the bush.

LULA. This is Saturday, tomorrow Sunday . . . thank Gawd for Monday; back to the army. That's one thing . . . Army keeps you off the street. (*The sound of the* SHRIMP MAN *passing in the street.*)

SHRIMP MAN. (*Offstage.*) Shrimp-dee-raw . . . I got raw shrimp. (NELSON *leaves the house just as* JULIA *steps out on her porch to hang a rug over the rail.* TEETA *enters* GREEN *house.*)

NELSON. Er . . . howdy-do, er . . . beg pardon. My name is Nelson. Lula Green's son, if you don't mind. Miss . . . er . . . Mrs.?

JULIA. (*After a brief hesitation.*) Miss . . . Julia Augustine.

NELSON. Miss Julia, you the best-lookin' woman I ever seen in my life. I declare you look jus' like a violin sounds. And I'm not talkin' 'bout pretty. You look like you got all the right feelin's, you know?

JULIA. Well, thank you, Mr. Nelson.

NELSON. See, you got me talkin' all outta my head. (LULA *enters,* TEETA *follows eating a biscuit and carrying a milk pail . . . she exits toward street.*) Let's go for a walk this evenin', get us a lemon phosphate.

JULIA. Oh, I don't care for any, Mr. Nelson.

LULA. That's right. She say stay home.

JULIA. (*To* NELSON.) I'm sorry.

NELSON. Don't send me back to the army feelin' bad 'cause you turn me down. Orange-ade tonight on your porch. I'll buy the oranges, you be the sugar.

JULIA. No, thank you.

NELSON. Let's make it—say—six o'clock.

JULIA. No, I said no!

LULA. Nelson, go see your friends. (*He waves goodbye to* JULIA *and exits through the back entry.*) He's got a lady friend, her name is Merrilee Jones. And he was just tryin' to be neighborly. That's how me and Nelson do. But you go on and stay to yourself. (*Starts toward her house.*)

JULIA. Miss Lula! I'm sorry I hurt your feelin's. Miss Lula! I have a gentleman friend, that's why I said no.

LULA. I didn't think-a that. When yall plan to cut the cake?

JULIA. Not right now. You see . . . when you offend Gawd you hate for it to be known. Gawd might forgive but people never will. I mean . . . when a man and a woman are not truly married . . .

LULA. Oh, I see.

JULIA. I live by myself . . . but he visits . . . I declare I don't know how to say . . .

LULA. Everybody's got some sin, but if it troubles your heart you're a gentle sinner, just a good soul gone wrong.

JULIA. That's a kind thought.

LULA. My husband, Gawd rest the dead, used to run 'round with other women; it made me kind-a careless with my life. One day, many long years ago, I was sittin' in a neighbor's house tellin' my troubles; my only child, my little boy, wandered out on the railroad track and got killed.

JULIA. That must-a left a fifty pound weight on your soul.

LULA. It did. But if we grow stronger . . . and rise higher than what's pullin' us down . . .

JULIA. Just like Climbin' Jacob's Ladder . . . (*Sings.*) Every round goes higher and higher . . .

LULA. Yes, rise higher than the dirt . . . that fifty pound weight will lift and you'll be free, free without anybody's by-your-leave. Do something to wash out the sin. That's why I got Nelson from the orphanage.

JULIA. And now you feel free?

LULA. No, not yet. But I believe Gawd wants me to start a new faith; one that'll make our days clear and easy to live. That's what I'm workin' on now. Oh, Miss Julia, I'm glad you my neighbor.

JULIA. Oh, thank you, Miss Lula! Sinners or saints, didn't Gawd give us a beautiful day this mornin'! (*The sound of cow-bells clanking and the thin piping of a tin and paper flute.* TEETA *backs into the yard carefully carrying the can of milk. The* BELL MAN *follows humming,* "*Over There*" *on the flute. He is a poor white about thirty years old but time has dealt him some hard blows. He carries a large suitcase; the American flag painted on both sides, cowbells are attached.* THE BELL MAN *rests his case on the ground. Fans with a very tired-looking handkerchief. He cuts the fool by dancing and singing a bit of a popular song as he turns corners around the yard.*)

THE BELL MAN. (*As* LULA *starts to go in the house.*) Stay where you at, Aunty! You used to live on Thompson Street. How's old Thompson Street?

JULIA. (*A slightly painful memory.*) I moved 'bout a year ago, moved to Queen Street.

THE BELL MAN. Move a lot, don'tcha? (*Opens suitcase.*) All right, everybody stay where you at! (*Goes into a fast sales spiel.*) Lace-trim ladies' drawers! Stockin's, ladies' stockin's . . . gottem for the knock-knees and the bow-legs too . . . white, black and navy blue! All right, no fools no fun! The joke's on me! Here we go! (*As he places some merchandise in front of the* WOMEN; *does a regular minstrel walk-around.*) Anything in the world . . . fifty cent a week and one long, sweet year to pay . . . Come on, little sister!

TEETA. (*Doing the walk-around with* THE BELL MAN.) And a-ring-ting-tang
And-a shimmy-she-bang
While the sun am a-shinin' and the sky am blue . . .
And a-ring-ting-tang
And-a shimmy-she-bang
While the sun am a-shinin' and the sky am blue . . .

LULA. (*Annoyed with* TEETA's *dancing with* THE BELL MAN.) Stop all that shimmy she-bang and get in the house! (*Swats at* TEETA *as she passes.*)

THE BELL MAN. (*Coldly.*) Whatcha owe me, Aunty?

LULA. Three dollars and ten cent. I don't have any money today.

THE BELL MAN. When you gon' pay?

LULA. Monday, or better say Wednesday.

JULIA. (*To divert his attention from* LULA.) How much for sheets?

THE BELL MAN. For you they on'y a dollar. (JULIA *goes to her house to get the money.* THE BELL MAN *moves toward her house as he talks to* LULA.) Goin' to the Service Men's parade Monday?

LULA. Yes, sir. My boy's marchin'. (*She exits.*)

THE BELL MAN. Uh-huh, I'll getcha later. Lord, Lord, Lord, how'dja like to trot 'round in the sun beggin' the poorest people in the world to buy somethin' from you. This is nice. Real nice. (*To* JULIA.) A good friend-a mine was a nigra boy. Me 'n' him was jus' like that. Fine fella, he couldn't read and he couldn't write.

JULIA. (*More to herself than to him.*) When he learns you're gon' lose a friend.

THE BELL MAN. But talkin' serious, what is race and

color? Put a paper bag over your head and who'd know the difference. Tryin' to remember me ain'tcha. I seen you one time coming out that bakery shop on Thompson Street, didn' see me.

JULIA. Is that so?

THE BELL MAN. (*Sits on the bed and bounches up and down.*) Awwww, Great Gawd-a-mighty! I haven't been on a high-built bed since I left the back woods.

JULIA. Please don't sit on my bed!

THE BELL MAN. Old country boy, that's me! Strong and healthy country boy . . . (*Not noticing any rejection.*) Sister, Um in need for it like I never been before. Will you 'comodate me? Straighten me, fix me up, will you? Wouldn't take but five minutes. Um quick like a jack rabbit. Wouldn't nobody know but you and me. (*She backs away from him as he pants and wheezes out his admiration.*) Um clean, too. Clean as the . . . Board-a Health. Don't believe in dippin' inta everything. I got no money now, but Ladies always need stockin's.

JULIA. (*Trying to keep her voice down, throws money at his feet.*) Get out of my house! Beneath contempt, that's what you are.

THE BELL MAN. Don't be lookin' down your nose at me . . . actin' like you Mrs. Martha Washington . . . Throwin' one chicken-shit dollar at me and goin' on . . .

JULIA. (*Picking up wooden clothes hanger.*) Get out! Out, before I take a stick to you.

THE BELL MAN. (*Bewildered, gathering his things to leave.*) Hell, what I care who you sleep with! It's your nooky! Give it way how you want to. I don't own no run-down bakery shop but I'm good as those who do. A baker ain' nobody . . .

JULIA. I wish you was dead, you just oughta be dead, stepped on and dead.

THE BELL MAN. Bet that's what my mama said first time she saw me. I was a fourteenth child. Damn women! . . . that's all right . . . Gawd bless you, Gav'd be with you and let his light shine on you. I give you good for evil . . . God bless you! (*As he walks down the porch steps.*) She must be goin' crazy. Unfriendly, sick-minded bitch! (TEETA *enters from* LULA'S *house.* THE BELL MAN *takes a strainer from his pocket and gives it to* TEETA *with a great show of generosity.*) Here, little honey. You take this sample. You got nice manners.

TEETA. Thank you, you the kin'est person in the world. (THE BELL MAN *exits to the tune of clanking bells and* LULA *enters.*)

JULIA. I hate those kind-a people.

LULA. You mustn't hate white folks. Don'tcha believe in Jesus? He's white.

JULIA. I wonder if he believes in me.

LULA. Gawd says we must love everybody.

JULIA. Just lovin' and lovin', no matter what? There are days when I love, days when I hate.

FANNY. Mattie, Mattie, mail!

JULIA. Your love is worthless if nobody wants it. (FANNY *enters carrying a letter. She rushes over to* MATTIE'S *house.*)

FANNY. I had to pay the postman two cent. No stamp.

TEETA. (*Calls to* JULIA.) Letter from papa! Gimmie my mama's five cents!

FANNY. (*To* TEETA.) You gon' end your days in the Colored Women's Jailhouse. (PRINCESS, *a little girl, enters skipping and jumping. She hops, runs and leaps across the yard.* PRINCESS *is six years old.* TEETA *takes money from* JULIA'S *outstretched hand and gives it to* FANNY.)

TEETA. (*To* MATTIE.) Letter from Papa! Gotta pay two cent!

FANNY. Now I owe you three cent . . . or do you want me to read the letter? (PRINCESS *gets wilder and wilder, makes Indian war whoops.* TEETA *joins the noise-making. They climb porches and play follow-the-leader.* PRINCESS *finally lands on* JULIA'S *porch after peeping and prying into everything along the way.*)

PRINCESS. (*Laughing merrily.*) Hello . . . hello . . . hello.

JULIA. (*Overwhelmed by the confusion.*) Well— Hello.

FANNY. Get away from my new tenant's porch!

PRINCESS. (*Is delighted with* FANNY'S *scolding and decides to mock her.*) My new tennis porch! (MATTIE *opens the letter and removes a ten dollar bill. Lost in thought she clutches the letter to her bosom.*)

FANNY. (*To* MATTIE.) Ought-a mind w-h-i-t-e children on w-h-i-t-e property!

PRINCESS. (*Now swinging on* JULIA'S *gate.*) . . . my new tennis porch!

FANNY. (*Chases* PRINCESS *around the yard.*) You Princess! Stop that! (JULIA *laughs but she is very near tears.*)

MATTIE. A letter from October.

FANNY. Who's gon' read it for you?

MATTIE. Lula!

PRINCESS. My new tennis porch!

FANNY. Princess! Mattie!

MATTIE. Teeta! In the house with that drat noise!

FANNY. It'll take Lula half-a day. (*Snatches letter.*) I won't charge but ten cent. (*Reads.*) "Dear, Sweet Molasses, My Darlin' Wife . . ."

MATTIE. No, I don't like how you make words sound. You read too rough. (*Sudden Offstage yells and screams from* TEETA *and* PRINCESS *as they struggle for possession of some toy.*)

PRINCESS. (*Offstage.*) Give it to me!

TEETA. No! It's mine!

MATTIE. (*Screams.*) Teeta! (*The* CHILDREN *are quiet.*)

FANNY. Dear, Sweet Molasses—how 'bout that?

JULIA. (*To* FANNY.) Stop that! Don't read her mail.

FANNY. She can't read it.

JULIA. She doesn't want to. She's gonna go on holdin' it in her hand and never know what's in it . . . just 'cause it's hers!

FANNY. Forgive 'em Father, they know not.

JULIA. Another thing, you told me it's quiet here! You call this quiet? I can't stand it!

FANNY. When you need me come and humbly knock on my *back* door. (*She exits.*)

MATTIE. (*Shouts to* FANNY.) I ain't gonna knock on no damn back door! Miss Julia, can you read? (*Offers the letter to* JULIA.) I'll give you some candy when I make it.

JULIA. (*Takes the letter.*) All right. (LULA *takes a seat to enjoy a rare social event. She winds stems for the paper flowers as* JULIA *reads.*) Dear, sweet molasses, my darlin' wife.

MATTIE. Yes, honey. (*To* JULIA.) Thank you.

JULIA. (*Reads.*) Somewhere, at sometime, on the high sea, I take my pen in hand . . . well, anyway, this undelible pencil.

LULA. Hope he didn't put it in his mouth.

JULIA. (*Reads.*) I be missin' you all the time.

MATTIE. And we miss you.

JULIA. (*Reads.*) Sorry we did not have our picture taken.

MATTIE. Didn't have the money.

JULIA. (*Reads.*) Would like to show one to the men and say this is my wife and child . . . They always be showin' pictures.

MATTIE. (*Waves the ten dollar bill.*) I'm gon' send you one, darlin'.

JULIA. (*Reads.*) I recall how we used to take a long walk on Sunday afternoon . . . (*Thinks about this for a moment.*) . . . then come home and be lovin' each other.

MATTIE. I recall.

JULIA. (*Reads.*) The Government people held up your allotment.

MATTIE. Oh, do Jesus.

JULIA. (*Reads.*) They have many papers to be sign, pink, blue and white also green. Money can't be had 'til all papers match. Mine don't match.

LULA. Takes a-while.

JULIA. (*Reads.*) Here is ten cash dollars I hope will not be stole.

MATTIE. (*Holds up the money.*) I got it.

JULIA. (*Reads.*) Go to Merchant Marine office and push things from your end.

MATTIE. Monday. Lula, le's ɡᴏ Monday.

LULA. I gotta see Nelson march in the parade.

JULIA. (*Reads.*) They say people now droppin' in the street, dying' from this war-time influenza. Don't get sick —buy tonic if you do. I love you.

MATTIE. Gotta buy a bottle-a tonic.

JULIA. (*Reads.*) Sometimes people say hurtful things 'bout what I am, like color and race . . .

MATTIE. Tell 'em you my brown-skin Carolina daddy, that's who the hell you are. Wish I was there.

JULIA. (*Reads.*) I try not to hear 'cause I do want to get back to your side. Two things a man can give the woman he loves . . . his name and his protection . . . The first you have, the last is yet to someday come. The war is here, the road is rocky. I am *ever* your lovin' husband, October.

MATTIE. So-long, darlin'. I wish I had your education.

JULIA. I only went through eighth grade. Name and protection. I know you love him.

MATTIE. Yes'm, I do. If I was to see October in bed with another woman, I'd never doubt him 'cause I trust him more than I do my own eyesight. Bet yall don't believe me.

JULIA. I know how much a woman can love. (*Glances at the letter again.*) Two things a man ran give . . .

MATTIE. Name and protection. That's right, too. I wouldn't live with no man. Man got to marry me. Man that won't marry you thinks nothin' of you. Just usin' you.

JULIA. I've never allowed anybody to *use* me!

LULA. (*Trying to move her away Stage Right.*) Mattie, look like rain.

MATTIE. A man can't use a woman less she let him.

LULA. (*To* MATTIE.) You never know when to stop.

JULIA. Well, I read your letter. Good day.

MATTIE. Did I hurtcha feelin's? Tell me, what'd I say.

JULIA. I—I've been keepin' company with someone for a long time and . . . we're not married.

MATTIE. For how long?

LULA. (*Half-heartedly tries to hush* MATTIE *but she would also like to know.*) Ohhh, Mattie.

JULIA. (*Without shame.*) Ten years today, ten full, faithful years.

MATTIE. He got a wife?

JULIA. (*Very tense and uncomfortable.*) No.

MATTIE. Oh, a man don't wanta get married, work on him. Cut off piece-a his shirt-tail and sew it to your petti-coat. It works. Get Fanny to read the tea leaves and tell you how to move. She's a old bitch but what she sees in a tea-cup is true.

JULIA. Thank you, Mattie.

LULA. Let's pray on it, Miss Julia. Gawd bring them together, in holy matrimony.

JULIA. Miss Lula, please don't . . . You know it's against the law for black and white to get married, so Gawd nor the tea leaves can help us. My friend is white and that's why I try to stay to myself. (*After a few seconds of silence.*)

LULA. Guess we shouldn't-a disturbed you.

JULIA. But I'm so glad you did. Oh, the things I can tell you 'bout bein' lonesome and shut-out. Always movin', one place to another, lookin' for some peace of mind. I moved out in the country . . . Pretty but quiet as the graveyard; so lonesome. One year I was in such a *lovely* colored neighborhood but they couldn't be bothered with me, you know? I've lived near sportin' people . . . they were very kindly but I'm not a sporty type person. Then I found this place hid way in the backyard so quiet, didn't see another soul . . . **And** that's why I thought yall wanted to tear my house down this mornin' . . . 'cause you might-a heard 'bout me and Herman . . . and some people are . . . well, they judge, they can't help judgin' you.

MATTIE. (*Eager to absolve her of wrong doing.*) Oh, darlin', we all do things we don't want sometimes. You grit your teeth and take all he's got; if you don't somebody else will.

LULA. No, no, you got no use for 'em so don't take nothin' from 'em.

MATTIE. He's takin' somethin' from her.

LULA. Have faith, you won't starve.

MATTIE. Rob him blind. Take it all. Let him froth at the mouth. Let him die in the poorhouse—bitter, bitter to the gone!

LULA. A white man is somethin' else. Everybody knows how that low-down slave master sent for a different black woman every night . . . for his pleasure. That's why none of us is the same color.

MATTIE. And right now today they're mean, honey. They can't help it; their nose is pinched together so close they can't get enough air. It makes 'em mean. And their mouth is set back in their face so hard and flat . . . no roundness, no sweetness, they can't even carry a tune.

LULA. I couldn't stand one of 'em to touch me intimate no matter what he'd give me.

JULIA. Miss Lula, you don't understand. Mattie, the way you and your husband feel that's the way it is with me 'n' Herman. He loves me . . . We love each other, that's all, we just love each other. (*After a split second of silence.*) And someday, as soon as we're able, we have to leave here and go where it's right . . . Where it's legal for everybody to marry. That's what we both want . . . to be man and wife—like you and October.

LULA. Well I have to cut out six dozen paper roses today. (*Starts for her house.*)

MATTIE. And I gotta make a batch-a candy and look after Princess so I can feed me and Teeta 'til October comes back. Thanks for readin' the letter. (*She enters her house.*)

JULIA. But Mattie, Lula—I wanted to tell you why it's been ten years—and why we haven't—

LULA. Good day, Miss Julia. (*Enters her house.*)

JULIA. Well, that's always the way. What am I doing standin' in a backyard explainin' my life? Stay to yourself, Julia Augustine. Stay to yourself. (*Sweeps her front porch.*)

I got to climb my way to glory
Got to climb it by myself
Ain't nobody here can climb it for me
I got to climb it for myself.

CURTAIN

ACT ONE

SCENE 2

TIME: *That evening. Cover closed Scene 1 curtain with song and laughter from* MATTIE, LULA *and* KIDS.

As curtain opens, JULIA *has almost finished the unpacking. The room now looks quite cozy. Once in a while she watches the clock and looks out of the window.* TEETA *follows* PRINCESS *out of* MATTIE'S *house and ties her sash.* PRINCESS *is holding a jump-rope.*

MATTIE. (*Offstage. Sings.*)
My best man left me, it sure do grieve my mind
When I'm laughin', I'm laughin' to keep from cryin' . . .

PRINCESS. (*Twirling the rope to one side.*) Ching, ching, China-man eat dead rat . . .

TEETA. (*As* PRINCESS *jumps rope.*) Knock him in the head with a baseball bat . . .

PRINCESS. You wanta jump?

TEETA. Yes.

PRINCESS. Say "Yes, Mam."

TEETA. No.

PRINCESS. Why?

TEETA. You too little.

PRINCESS. (*Takes bean bag from her pocket.*) You can't play with my bean-bag.

TEETA. I 'on care, play it by yourself.

PRINCESS. (*Drops rope, tosses the bag to* TEETA.) Catch. (TEETA *throws it back.* HERMAN *appears at the back-entry. He is a strong, forty year old working man. His light brown hair is sprinkled with gray. At the present moment he is tired.* PRINCESS *notices him because she is facing the back fence. He looks for a gate or opening but can find none.*) Hello.

TEETA. Mama! Mama!

HERMAN. Hello, children. Where's the gate? (HERMAN *passes several packages through a hole in the fence; he thinks of climbing the fence but it is very rickety. He disappears from view.* MATTIE *dashes out of her house, notices the packages, runs into* LULA'S *house, then back into the yard.* LULA *enters in a flurry of excitement; gathers a couple of pieces from the clothesline.* MATTIE *goes to inspect the packages.*)

LULA. Don't touch 'em, Mattie. Might be dynamite.

MATTIE. Well, I'm gon' get my head blowed off, 'cause I wanta see. (NELSON *steps out wearing his best civilian clothes; neat fitting suit, striped silk shirt and bulldog shoes in ox-blood leather. He claps his hands to frighten* MATTIE.)

MATTIE. Oh, look at him. Where's the party?

NELSON. Everywhere! The ladies have heard Nelson's home. They waitin' for me!

LULA. Don't get in trouble. Don't answer anybody that bothers you.

NELSON. How come it is that when I carry a sack-a coal on my back you don't worry, but when I'm goin' out to enjoy myself you almost go crazy.

LULA. Go on! Deliver the piece to the funeral. (*Hands him a funeral piece.* MATTIE *proceeds to examine the contents of a paper bag.*)

NELSON. Fact is, I was gon' stay home and have me some orange drink, but Massa beat me to it. None-a my business no-how, dammit. (MATTIE *opens another bag.* HERMAN *enters through the front entry.* FANNY *follows at a respectable distance.*)

MATTIE. Look, rolls and biscuits!

LULA. Why'd he leave the food in the yard?

HERMAN. Because I couldn't find the gate. Good evening. Pleasant weather. Howdy do. Cool this evenin'. (*Silence.*) Err—I see where the Allies suffered another set-back yesterday. Well, that's the war, as they say. (*The* WOMEN *answers with nods and vague throat clearings.* JULIA *opens her door, he enters.*)

MATTIE. That's the lady's husband. He's a light colored man.

PRINCESS. What is a light colored man? (*Children exit with* MATTIE *and* NELSON. FANNY *exits by front entry,* LULA *to her house.*)

JULIA. Why'd you pick a conversation? I tell you 'bout that.

HERMAN. Man gotta say somethin' stumblin' round in a strange back yard.

JULIA. Why didn't you wear your good suit? You know how people like to look you over and sum you up.

HERMAN. Mama and Annabelle made me so damn mad tonight. When I got home Annabelle had this in the window. (*Removes a cardboard sign from the bag . . . printed with red, white and blue crayon . . .* WE ARE AMERICAN CITIZENS . . .)

JULIA. We are American Citizens. Why'd she put it in the window?

HERMAN. Somebody wrote cross the side of our house in purple paint . . . "Krauts . . . Germans live here"! I'd-a broke his arm if I caught him.

JULIA. It's the war. Makes people mean. But didn't she print it pretty.

HERMAN. Comes from Mama boastin' 'bout her German grandfather, now it's no longer fashionable. I snatched that coward sign outta the window . . . Goddamit, I says . . . Annabelle cryin', Mama hollerin' at her. Gawd save us from the ignorance, I say . . . Why should I see a sign in the window when I get home? That Annabelle got flags flyin' in the front yard, the backyard . . . and red, white and blue flowers in the grass . . . confound nonsense . . . Mama is an ignorant woman . . .

JULIA. Don't say that . . .

HERMAN. A poor ignorant woman who is mad because she was born a sharecropper . . . outta her mind 'cause she ain't high class society. We're red-neck crackers, I told her, that's what.

JULIA. Oh, Herman . . . no you didn't . . .

HERMAN. I did.

JULIA. (*Standing.*) But she raised you . . . loaned you all-a-her three thousand dollars to pour into that bakery shop. You know you care about her.

HERMAN. Of course I do. But sometimes she makes me so mad . . . Close the door, lock out the world . . . all of 'em that ain't crazy are coward. (*Looks at sign.*) Poor Annabelle—Miss War-time Volunteer . . .

JULIA. She's what you'd call a very Patriotic Person, wouldn't you say?

HERMAN. Well, guess it is hard for her to have a brother who only makes pies in time of war.

JULIA. A brother who makes pies and loves a nigger!

HERMAN. Sweet Kerist, there it is again!

JULIA. Your mama's own words . . . according to you —I'll never forget them as long as I live. Annabelle, you've got a brother who makes pies and loves a nigger.

HERMAN. How can you remember seven or eight years ago, for Gawd's sake? Sorry I told it.

JULIA. I'm not angry, honeybunch, dear heart. I just remember.

HERMAN. When you say honeybunch, you're angry. Where do you want your Aunt Cora?

JULIA. On my dresser!

HERMAN. An awful mean woman.

JULIA. Don't get me started on your mama and Annabelle. (*Pause.*)

HERMAN. Julia, why did you move into a backyard?

JULIA. (*Goes to him.*) Another move, another mess. Sometimes I feel like fightin' . . . and there's nobody to fight but you . . .

HERMAN. Open the box. Go on. Open it.

JULIA. (*Opens the box and reveals a small but ornate wedding cake with a bride and groom on top and ten pink candles.*) Ohhh, it's the best one ever. Tassels, bells, roses . . .

HERMAN. . . . Daffodils and silver sprinkles . . .

JULIA. You're the best baker in the world.

HERMAN. (*As he lights the candles.*) Because you put up with me . . .

JULIA. Gawd knows that.

HERMAN. . . . because the palms of your hands and the soles of your feet are pink and brown . . .

JULIA. Jus' listen to him. Well, go on.

HERMAN. Because you're a good woman, a kind, good woman.

JULIA. Thank you very much, Herman.

HERMAN. Because you care about me.

JULIA. Well, I do.

HERMAN. Happy ten years . . . Happy tenth year.

JULIA. And the same to you.

HERMAN. (*Tries a bit of soft barbershop harmony.*) I love you as I never loved before (JULIA *joins him.*) When first I met you on the village green Come to me e'er my dream of love is o'er I love you as I loved you When you were sweet— Take the end up higher— When you were su-weet six-ateen. Now blow! (*They blow out the candles and kiss through a cloud of smoke.*)

JULIA. (*Almost forgetting something.*) Got something for you. Because you were my only friend when Aunt

Cora sent me on a sleep-in job in the white-folks kitchen.
And wasn't that Miss Bessie one mean white woman?
(*Gives present to* HERMAN.)

HERMAN. Oh, Julia, just say she was mean.

JULIA. Well yes, but she was white too.

HERMAN. A new peel, thank you. A new pastry bag.
Thank you.

JULIA. (*She gives him a sweater.*) I did everything
right but one arm came out shorter.

HERMAN. That's how I feel. Since three o'clock this
morning, I turned out twenty ginger breads, thirty sponge
cakes, lady fingers, Charlotte Russe . . . loaf bread,
round bread, twist bread and water rolls . . . and—

JULIA. Tell me about pies. Do pies!

HERMAN. Fifty pies. Open apple, closed apple, apple-
crumb, sweet potato and pecan. And I got a order for a
large wedding cake. They want it in the shape of a battleship. (HERMAN *gives* JULIA *ring box.* JULIA *takes out a
wide, gold wedding band—it is strung on a chain.*) It's
a wedding band . . . on a chain . . . To have until
such time as . . . It's what you wanted, Julia. A damn
fool present.

JULIA. Sorry I lost your graduation ring. If you'd-a
gone to college what do you think you'd-a been?

HERMAN. A baker with a degree.

JULIA. (*Reads.*) Herman and Julia 1908 . . . and now
it's . . . 1918. Time runs away. A wedding band . . .
on a chain. (*She fastens the chain around her neck.*)

HERMAN. A damn fool present. (JULIA *drops the ring
inside of her dress.*)

JULIA. It comforts me. It's your promise. You hungry?

HERMAN. No.

JULIA. After the war, the people across the way are
goin' to Philadelphia.

HERMAN. I hear it's cold up there. People freeze to
death waitin' for a trolley car.

JULIA. (*Leans back beside him, rubs his head.*) In the

middle of the night a big bird flew cryin' over this house— Then he was gone, the way time goes flyin' . . .

HERMAN. Julia, why did you move in a back yard? Out in the country the air was so sweet and clean. Makes me feel shame . . .

JULIA. (*Rubbing his back.*) Crickets singin' that lonesome evenin' song. Any kind-a people better than none a-tall.

HERMAN. Mama's beggin' me to hire Greenlee again, to help in the shop, "Herman, sit back like a half-way gentleman and just take in money."

JULIA. Greenlee! When white-folks decide . . .

HERMAN. People, Julia, people.

JULIA. When people decide to give other people a job, they come up with the biggest Uncle Tom they can find. The *people* I know call him a "white-folks-nigger." It's a terrible expression so don't you ever use it.

HERMAN. He seems dignified, Julia.

JULIA. Jus' 'cause you're clean and stand straight, that's not dignity. Even speakin' nice might not be dignity.

HERMAN. What's dignity? Tell me. Do it.

JULIA. Well, it . . . it . . . It's a feeling— It's a spirit that rises higher than the dirt around it, without any by-your-leave. It's not proud and it's not 'shamed . . . Dignity "Is" . . . and it's never Greenlee . . . I don't know if it's us either, honey.

HERMAN. (*Standing.*) It still bothers my mother that I'm a baker. "When you gonna rise in the world!" A baker who rises . . . (*Laughs and coughs a little.*) Now she's worried 'bout Annabelle marryin' a sailor. After all, Annabelle is a concert pianist. She's had only one concert . . . in a church . . . and not many people there.

JULIA. A sailor might just perservere and become an admiral. Yes, an admiral and a concert pianist.

HERMAN. Ten years. If I'd-a known what I know now, I wouldn't-a let Mama borrow on the house or give me the bakery.

JULIA. Give what? Three broken stoves and all-a your papa's unpaid bills.

HERMAN. I *got* to pay her back. And I can't go to Philadelphia or wherever the hell you're saying to go. I can hear you thinkin', Philadelphia, Philadelphia, Phil . . .

JULIA. (*Jumping up. Pours wine.*) Oh damnation! The hell with that!

HERMAN. All right, not so much hell and damn. When we first met you were so shy.

JULIA. Sure was, wouldn't say "dog" 'cause it had a tail. In the beginnin' nothin' but lovin' and kissin' . . . and thinkin' 'bout you. Now I worry 'bout gettin' old. I do. Maybe you'll meet somebody younger. People do get old, y'know. (*Sits on bed.*)

HERMAN. There's an old couple 'cross from the bakery . . . "Mabel," he yells, "Where's my keys!" . . . Mabel has a big behind on her. She wears his carpet slippers. "All right, Robbie, m'boy," she says . . . Robbie walks kinda one-sided. But they're havin' a pretty good time. We'll grow old together both of us havin' the same name. (*Takes her in his arms.*) Julia, I love yóu . . . you know it . . . I love you . . . (*After a pause.*) Did you have my watch fixed?

JULIA. (*Sleepily.*) Uh-huh, it's in my purse. (*Getting up.*) Last night when the bird flew over the house—I dreamed 'bout the devil's face in the fire . . . He said "I'm comin' to drag you to hell."

HERMAN. (*Sitting up.*) There's no other hell, honey. Celestine was sayin' the other day—

JULIA. How do you know what Celestine says?

HERMAN. Annabelle invited her to dinner.

JULIA. They still trying to throw that white widow-woman at you? Oh, Herman, I'm gettin' mean . . . jumpin' at noises . . . and bad dreams.

HERMAN. (*Brandishing bottle.*) Dammit, this is the big bird that flew over the house!

JULIA. I don't go anywhere, I don't know anybody, I gotta do somethin'. Sometimes I need to have company—

to say . . . "Howdy-do, pleasant evenin,' do drop in."
Sometimes I need other people. How you ever gonna pay
back three thousand dollars? Your side hurt?

HERMAN. Schumann, came in to see me this mornin'.
Says he'll buy me out, ten cents on the dollar, and give
me a job bakin' for him . . . it's an offer,—can get
seventeen hundred cash.

JULIA. Don't do it, Herman. That sure wouldn't be
dignity.

HERMAN. He makes an American flag outta ginger-
bread. But they sell. Bad taste sells. Julia, where do you
want to go? New York, Philadelphia, where? Let's try
their dignity. Say where you want to go.

JULIA. Well, darlin', if folks are freezin' in Philadelphia, we'll go to New York.

HERMAN. Right! You go and size up the place. Mean-
while I'll stay here and do like everybody else, make war
money . . . battleship cakes, cannon-ball cookies . . .
chocolate bullets . . . they'll sell. Pay my debts. Less
than a year, I'll be up there with money in my pockets.

JULIA. Northerners talk funny— "We're from New
Yo*rrr*k."

HERMAN. I'll getcha train ticket next week.

JULIA. No train. I wanta stand on the deck of a Clyde
Line boat, wavin' to the people on the shore. The whistle blowin', flags flyin' . . . wavin' my handkerchief . . .
So long, so long, look here—South Carolina . . . so long,
hometown . . . goin' away by myself— (*Tearfully blows
her nose.*)

HERMAN. You gonna like it. Stay with your cousin and
don't talk to strangers. (JULIA *gets dress from her hope
chest.*)

JULIA. Then, when we do get married we can have a
quiet reception. My cut glass punch bowl . . . little
sandwiches, a few friends . . . Herman? Hope my weddin' dress isn't too small. It's been waitin' a good while.
(*Holds dress in front of her.*) I'll use all of my hope

chest things. Quilts, Irish linens, the silver cups . . . Oh, Honey, how are you gonna manage with me gone?

HERMAN. Buy warm underwear and a woolen coat with a fur collar . . . to turn against the northern wind. What size socks do I wear?

JULIA. Eleven, eleven and a half if they run small.

HERMAN. . . . what's the store? Write it down.

JULIA. Coleridge. And go to King Street for your shirts.

HERMAN. Coleridge. Write it down.

JULIA. Keep payin' Ruckheiser, the tailor, so he can start your new suit.

HERMAN. Ruckheiser. Write it down.

JULIA. Now that I know I'm goin' we can take our time.

HERMAN. No, rush, hurry, make haste, do it. Look at you . . . like your old self.

JULIA. No, no, not yet—I'll go soon as we get around to it. (*Kisses him.*)

HERMAN. That's right. Take your time . . .

JULIA. Oh, Herman. (MATTIE *enters through the back gate with* TEETA. *She pats and arranges* TEETA'S *hair.* FANNY *enters from the front entry and goes to* JULIA'S *window.*)

MATTIE. You goin' to Lula's service?

FANNY. A new faith. Rather be a Catholic than somethin' you gotta make up. Girl, my new tenant and her—

MATTIE. (*Giving* FANNY *the high-sign to watch what she says in front of* TEETA.) . . . and her husband.

FANNY. I gotcha. She and her husband was in there havin' a orgy. Singin', laughin', screamin', cryin' . . . I'd like to be a fly on that wall. (LULA *enters the yard wearing a shawl over her head and a red band on her arm. She carries two chairs and places them beside two kegs.*)

LULA. Service time! (MATTIE, TEETA *and* FANNY *enter the yard and sit down.* LULA *places a small table and a cross.*)

FANNY. (*Goes to* JULIA'S *door and knocks.*) Let's

spread the word to those who need it. (*Shouts.*) Miss Julia, don't stop if you in the middle-a somethin'. We who love Gawd are gatherin' for prayer. Got any time for Jesus?

ALL. (*Sing.*) When the roll is called up yonder.

JULIA. Thank you, Miss Fanny. (FANNY *flounces back to her seat in triumph.* JULIA *sits on the bed near* HERMAN.)

HERMAN. Dammit, she's makin' fun of you.

JULIA. (*Smooths her dress and hair.*) Nobody's invited me anywhere in a long time . . . so I'm goin'.

HERMAN. (*Standing.*) I'm gonna buy you a Clyde Line ticket for New York City on Monday . . . this Monday.

JULIA. Monday?

HERMAN. As Gawd is my judge. That's dignity. Monday.

JULIA. (*Joyfully kissing him.*) Yes, Herman! (*She enters yard.*)

LULA. My form-a service opens with praise. Let us speak to Gawd.

MATTIE. Well, I thang Gawd that—that I'm livin' and I pray my husband comes home safe.

TEETA. I love Jesus and Jesus loves me.

ALL. Amen.

FANNY. I thang Gawd that I'm able to rise spite-a those who try to hold me down, spite-a those who are two-faceted, spite-a those in my own race who jealous 'cause I'm doin' so much better than the rest of 'em. He preparest a table for me in the presence of my enemies. Double-deal Fanny Johnson all you want but me 'n' Gawd's gonna come out on top. (ALL *look to* JULIA.)

JULIA. I'm sorry for past sin—but from Monday on through eternity—I'm gonna live in dignity accordin' to the laws of God and man. Oh, Glory!

LULA. Glory Hallelujah! (NELSON *enters a bit unsteadily . . . struts and preens while singing.*)

NELSON. Come here black woman . . . whoooo . . . eee . . . on daddy's knee . . . etc.

LULA. (*Trying to interrupt him.*) We're testifyin . . .

NELSON. (*Throwing hat on porch.*) Right! Testify! Tonight I asked the prettiest girl in Carolina to be my wife; And Merrilee Jones told me . . . I'm sorry but you got nothin to offer. She's right! I got nothin to offer but a hard way to go. Merrilee Jones . . . workin for the rich white folks and better off washin their dirty drawers than marryin me.

LULA. Respect the church! (*Slaps him.*)

NELSON. (*Sings.*) Come here, black woman (etc.) . . .

JULIA. Oh, Nelson, respect your mother!

NELSON. Respect your damn self, Julia Augustine! (*Continues singing.*)

LULA. How we gonna find a new faith?

NELSON. (*Softly.*) By tellin' the truth, Mamma. Merrilee ain't no liar. I got nothin' to offer, just like October.

MATTIE. You keep my husband's name outta your mouth.

NELSON. (*Sings.*) Come here, black woman . . .

FANNY AND CONGREGATION. (*Sing.*)

Ain't gon let nobody turn me round, turn me round, turn me round

Ain't gon let nobody turn me round . . .

HERMAN. (*Staggers out to porch.*) Julia, I'm going now, I'm sorry . . . I don't feel well . . . I don't know . . . (*Slides forward and falls.*)

JULIA. Mr. Nelson . . . won'tcha please help me . . .

FANNY. Get him out of my yard. (NELSON *and* JULIA *help* HERMAN *in to bed. Others freeze in yard.*)

END OF ACT ONE

ACT TWO

Scene 1

TIME: *Sunday morning.*

SCENE: *The same as Act One except the yard and houses are neater. The clothes line is down. Off in the distance someone is humming a snatch of a hymn. Church bells are ringing.* HERMAN *is in a heavy, restless sleep. The bed covers indicate he has spent a troubled night. On the table* D. R. *are medicine bottles, cups and spoons.* JULIA *is standing beside the bed, swinging a steam kettle, she stops and puts it on a trivet on top of her hope chest.*

FANNY. (*Seeing her.*) Keep usin' the steam-kettle. (HERMAN *groans lightly.*)

MATTIE. (*Picks up scissors.*) Put the scissors under the bed, open. It'll cut the pain.

FANNY. (*Takes scissors from* MATTIE.) That's for childbirth.

JULIA. He's had too much paregoric. Sleepin' his life away. I want a doctor.

FANNY. Over my dead body. It's against the damn law for him to be layin' up in a black woman's bed.

MATTIE. A doctor will call the police.

FANNY. They'll say I run a bad house.

JULIA. I'll tell 'em the truth.

MATTIE. We don't tell things to police.

FANNY. When Lula gets back with his sister, his damn sister will take charge.

MATTIE. That's his family.

FANNY. Family is family.

JULIA. I'll hire a hack and take him to a doctor.

FANNY. He might die on you. That's police. That's the work-house.

JULIA. I'll say I found him on the street!

FANNY. Walk into the jaws of the law—they'll chew you up.

JULIA. Suppose his sister won't come?

FANNY. She'll be here. (FANNY *picks up a tea-cup and turns it upside down on the saucer and twirls it.*) I see a ship, a ship sailin' on the water.

MATTIE. Water clear or muddy?

FANNY. Crystal clear.

MATTIE. (*Realizing she's late.*) Oh, I gotta get Princess so her folks can open their ice cream parlor. Take care-a Teeta.

FANNY. I see you on your way to Miami, Florida, goin' on a trip.

JULIA. (*Sitting on window seat.*) I know you want me to move. I will, Fanny.

FANNY. Julia, it's hard to live under these mean white-folks . . . but I've done it. I'm the first and only colored they let buy land 'round here.

JULIA. They all like you, Fanny. Only one of 'em cares for me . . . just one.

FANNY. Yes, I'm thought highly of. When I pass by they can say . . . "There she go, Fanny Johnson, rep-presentin' her race in-a approved manner" . . . 'cause they don't have to worry 'bout my next move. I can't afford to mess that up on account-a you or any-a the rest-a these hard-luck, better-off-dead, triflin' niggers.

JULIA. (*Crossing up Right.*) I'll move. But I'm gonna call a doctor.

FANNY. Do it, we'll have a yellow quarantine sign on the front door . . . "INFLUENZA". Doctor'll fill out papers for the law . . . address . . . race . . .

JULIA. I . . . I guess I'll wait until his sister gets here.

FANNY. No, you call a doctor, Nelson won't march in

the parade tomorrow or go back to the army, Mattie'll be outta work, Lula can't deliver flowers . . .

JULIA. I'm sorry, so very sorry. I'm the one breakin' laws, doin' wrong.

FANNY. I'm not judgin' you. High or low, nobody's against this if it's kept quiet. But when you pickin' white . . . pick a wealthy white. It makes things easier.

JULIA. No, Herman's not rich and I've never tried to beat him out of anything.

FANNY. (*Crossing to* JULIA.) Well, he just ought-a be and you just should-a. A colored woman needs money more than anybody else in this world.

JULIA. You sell yours.

FANNY. All I don't sell I'm going to keep.

HERMAN. Julia?

FANNY. (*Very genial.*) Well, well, sir, how you feelin', Mr. Herman? This is Aunt Fanny . . . Miss Julia's landlady. You lookin' better, Mr. Herman. We've been praying for you. (FANNY *exits to* TEETA'S *house.*)

JULIA. Miss Lula—went to get your sister.

HERMAN. Why?

JULIA. Fanny made me. We couldn't wake you up. (*He tries to sit up in bed to prepare for leaving. She tries to help him. He falls back on the pillow.*)

HERMAN. Get my wallet . . . see how much money is there. What's that smell? (*She takes the wallet from his coat pocket. She completes counting the money.*)

JULIA. Eucalyptus oil, to help you breathe; I smell it, you smell it and Annabelle will have to smell it too! Seventeen dollars.

HERMAN. A boat ticket to New York is fourteen dollars— Ohhhh, Kerist! Pain . . . pain . . . Count to ten . . . one, two . . . (JULIA *gives paregoric water to him. He drinks. She puts down glass and picks up damp cloth from bowl on tray and wipes his brow.*) My mother is made out of too many . . . little things . . . the price of carrots, how much fat is on the meat . . . little things make people small. Make ignorance—y'know?

JULIA. Don't fret about your people, I promise I won't be surprised at anything and I won't have unpleasant words no matter what.

HERMAN. (*The pain eases. He is exhausted.*) Ahhh, there . . . All men are born which is—utterly untrue. (*NELSON steps out of the house. He is brushing his army jacket. HERMAN moans slightly. JULIA gets her dressmaking scissors and opens them, places the scissors under the bed.*)

FANNY. (*To NELSON as she nods towards JULIA's house.*) I like men of African descent, myself.

NELSON. Pitiful people. They pitiful.

FANNY. They common. Only reason I'm sleepin' in a double bed by myself is 'cause I got to bear the standard for the race. I oughta run her outta here for the sake-a the race too.

NELSON. It's your property. Run us all off it, Fanny.

FANNY. Plenty-a these hungry, jobless, bad-luck colored men, just-a itchin' to move in on my gravy-train. I don't want 'em.

NELSON. (*With good nature.*) Right, Fanny! We empty-handed, got nothin' to offer.

FANNY. But I'm damn tired-a ramblin' round in five rooms by myself. House full-a new furniture, the icebox forever full-a goodies. I'm a fine cook and I know how to pleasure a man . . . he wouldn't have to step outside for a thing . . . food, fun and finance . . . all under one roof. Nelson, how'd you like to be my business advisor? Fix you up a little office in my front parlor. You wouldn't have to work for white folks . . . and Lula wouldn't have to pay rent. The war won't last forever . . . then what you gonna do? They got nothin' for you but haulin' wood and cleanin' toilets. Let's you and me pitch in together.

NELSON. I know you just teasin', but I wouldn't do a-tall. Somebody like me ain't good enough for you noway, but you a fine-lookin' woman, though. After the

war I might hit out for Chicago or Detroit . . . a rollin'
stone gathers no moss.

FANNY. Roll on. Just tryin' to help the race. (LULA
enters by front entry, followed by ANNABELLE, *a woman
in her thirties. She assumes a slightly mincing air of
fashionable delicacy. She might be graceful if she were
not ashamed of her size. She is nervous and fearful in
this strange atmosphere. The others fall silent as they see
her.* ANNABELLE *wonders if* PRINCESS *is her brother's
child? Or could it be* TEETA, *or both?*)

ANNABELLE. Hello there . . . er . . . children.

PRINCESS. (*Can't resist mocking her.*) Hello there, er
. . . children. (*Giggles.*)

ANNABELLE. (*To* TEETA.) Is she your sister? (ANNA-
BELLE *looks at* NELSON *and draws her shawl a little
closer.*)

TEETA. You have to ask my mama.

NELSON. (*Annoyed with* ANNABELLE'S *discomfort.*)
Mom, where's the flat-iron? (*Turns and enters his house.
LULA follows.* MATTIE *and* CHILDREN *exit.*)

FANNY. I'm the landlady. Mr. Herman had every care
and kindness 'cept a doctor. Miss Juliaaaa! That's the
family's concern. (FANNY *opens door, then exits.*)

ANNABELLE. Sister's here. It's Annabelle.

JULIA. (*Shows her to a chair.*) One minute he's with
you, the next he's gone. Paregoric makes you sleep.

ANNABELLE. (*Dabs at her eyes with a handkerchief.*)
Cryin' doesn't make sense a-tall. I'm a volunteer worker
at the Naval hospital . . . I've nursed my mother . . .
(*Chokes with tears.*)

JULIA. (*Pours a glass of water for her.*) Well, this is
more than sickness. It's not knowin' 'bout other things.

ANNABELLE. We've known for years. He is away all
the time and when old Uncle Greenlee . . . He's a
colored gentlemen who works in our neighborhood . . .
and he said . . . he told . . . er, well, people do talk.
(ANNABELLE *spills water,* JULIA *attempts to wipe the
water from her dress.*) Don't do that . . . It's all right.

HERMAN. Julia?

ANNABELLE. Sister's here. Mama and Uncle Greenlee have a hack down the street. Gets a little darker we'll take you home, call a physician . . .

JULIA. Can't you do it right away?

ANNABELLE. 'Course you could put him out. Please let us wait 'til dark.

JULIA. Get a doctor.

ANNABELLE. Our plans are made, thank you.

HERMAN. Annabelle, this is Julia.

ANNABELLE. Hush.

HERMAN. This is my sister.

ANNABELLE. Now be still.

JULIA. I'll call Greenlee to help him dress.

ANNABELLE. No. Dress first. The colored folk in *our* neighborhood have great respect for us.

HERMAN. Because I give away cinnamon buns, for Kerist sake.

ANNABELLE. (*To* JULIA.) I promised my mother I'd try and talk to you. Now—you look like one-a the nice coloreds . . .

HERMAN. Remember you are a concert pianist, that is a very dignified calling.

ANNABELLE. Put these on. We'll turn our backs.

JULIA. He can't.

ANNABELLE. (*Holds the covers in a way to keep his mid-section under wraps.*) Hold up. (*They manage to get the trousers up as high as his waist but they are twisted and crooked.*) Up we go! There . . . (*They are breathless from the effort of lifting him.*) Now fasten your clothing. (JULIA *fastens his clothes.*) I declare, even a dead man oughta have enough pride to fasten himself.

JULIA. You're a volunteer at the Naval hospital?

HERMAN. (*As another pain hits him.*) Julia, my little brown girl . . . Keep singing . . .

JULIA.
We are climbin' Jacob's ladder, We are climbin' Jacob's ladder,

We are climbin' Jacob's ladder, Soldier of the Cross . . .

HERMAN. The palms of your hands . . .

JULIA. (*Singing.*) Every round goes higher and higher . . .

HERMAN. . . . the soles of your feet are pink and brown.

ANNABELLE. Dammit, hush. Hush this noise. Sick or not sick, hush! It's ugliness. (*To* JULIA.) Let me take care of him, please, leave us alone.

JULIA. I'll get Greenlee.

ANNABELLE. No! You hear me? No.

JULIA. I'll be outside.

ANNABELLE. (*Sitting on bed.*) If she hadn't-a gone I'd-a screamed. (JULIA *stands on the porch.* ANNABELLE *cries.*) I thought so highly of you . . . and here you are in somethin' that's been festerin' for years. (*In disbelief.*) One of the finest women in the world is pinin' her heart out for you, a woman who's pure gold. Everything Celestine does for Mama she's really doin' for you . . . to get next to you . . . But even a Saint wants some reward.

HERMAN. I don't want Saint Celestine.

ANNABELLE. (*Standing.*) Get up! (*Tries to move* HERMAN.) At the Naval hospital I've seen influenza cases tied down to keep 'em from walkin'. What're we doin' here? How do you meet a black woman?

HERMAN. She came in the bakery on a rainy Saturday evening.

ANNABELLE. (*Giving in to curiosity.*) Yes?

MATTIE. (*Offstage. Scolding* TEETA *and* PRINCESS.) Sit down and drink that lemonade. Don't bother me!

HERMAN. "I smell rye bread baking." Those were the first words . . . Every day . . . Each time the bell sounds over the shop door I'm hopin' it's the brown girl . . . pretty shirt-waist and navy blue skirt. One day I took her hand . . . "little lady, don't be afraid of me" . . . She wasn't. . . . I've never been lonesome since.

ANNABELLE. (*Holding out his shirt.*) Here, your arm

goes in the sleeve. (*They're managing to get the shirt on.*)

HERMAN. (*Beginning to ramble.*) Julia? Your body is velvet . . . the sweet blackberry kisses . . . you are the night-time, the warm, Carolina night-time in my arms . . .

ANNABELLE. (*Bitterly.*) Most excitement I've ever had was takin' piano lessons.

JULIA. (*Calls from porch.*) Ready?

ANNABELLE. No. Rushin' us out. A little longer, please. (*Takes a comb from her purse and nervously combs his hair.*) You nor Mama put yourselves out to understand my Walter when I had him home to dinner. Yes, he's a common sailor . . . I wish he was an officer. I never liked a sailor's uniform, tight pants and middy blouses . . . but they are in the service of their country . . . He's taller than I am. You didn't even stay home that one Sunday like you promised. Must-a been chasin' after some-a them blackberry kisses you love so well. Mama made a jackass outta Walter. You know how she can do. He left lookin' like a whipped dog. Small wonder he won't live down here. I'm crazy-wild 'bout Walter even if he is a sailor. Marry Celestine. She'll take care-a Mama and I can go right on up to the Brooklyn Navy Yard. I been prayin' so hard . . . You marry Celestine and set me free. And Gawd knows I don't want another concert.

HERMAN. (*Sighs.*) Pain, keep singing.

ANNABELLE. Dum-dum-blue Danube. (*He falls back on the pillow. She bathes his head with a damp cloth.*)

JULIA. (*As NELSON enters the yard.*) Tell your mother I'm grateful for her kindness. I appreciate . . .

NELSON. Don't have so much to say to me. (*Quietly, in a straightforward manner.*) They set us on fire 'bout their women. String us up, pour on kerosene and light a match. Wouldn't I make a bright flame in my new uniform?

JULIA. Don't be thinkin' that way.

NELSON. I'm thinkin' 'bout black boys hangin' from trees in Little Mountain, Elloree, Winnsboro.

JULIA. Herman never killed anybody. I couldn't care 'bout that kind-a man.

NELSON. (*Stopping, turning to her.*) How can you account for carin' 'bout him a-tall?

JULIA. In that place where I worked, he was the only one who cared . . . who really cared. So gentle, such a gentle man . . . "Yes, Ma'am," . . . "No, Ma'am," "Thank you, Ma'am . . ." In the best years of my youth, my Aunt Cora sent me out to work on a sleep-in job. His shop was near that place where I worked. . . . Most folks don't have to *account* for why they love.

NELSON. You ain't most folks. You're down on the bottom with us, under his foot. A black man got nothin' to offer you . . .

JULIA. I wasn't lookin' for anybody to do for me.

NELSON. . . . and *he's* got nothin' to offer. The one layin' on your mattress, not even if he's kind as you say. He got nothin' for you . . . but some meat and gravy or a new petticoat . . . or maybe he can give you meriny-lookin' little bastard chirrun for us to take in and raise up. We're the ones who feed and raise 'em when it's like this . . . They don't want 'em. They only too glad to let us have their kin-folk. As it is, we supportin' half-a the slave-master's offspring right now.

JULIA. Go fight those who fight you. He never threw a pail-a water on you. Why didn't you fight them that did? Takin' it out on me 'n Herman 'cause you scared of 'em . . .

NELSON. Scared? What scared! If I gotta die I'm carryin' one 'long with me.

JULIA. No you not. You gon' keep on fightin' me.

NELSON. . . . Scared-a what? I look down on 'em, I spit on 'em.

JULIA. No, you don't. They throw dirty water on your uniform . . . and you spit on me!

NELSON. Scared, what scared!

JULIA. You fightin' me, me, me, not them . . . never them.

NELSON. Yeah, I was scared and I'm tougher, stronger,

a better man than any of 'em . . . but they won't letcha fight one or four or ten. I was scared to fight a hundred or a thousand. A losin' fight.

JULIA. I'd-a been afraid too.

NELSON. And you scared right now, you let the woman run you out your house.

JULIA. I didn't want to make trouble.

NELSON. But that's what a fight is . . . trouble.

LULA. (*In her doorway.*) Your mouth will kill you. (*To* JULIA.) Don't tell Mr. Herman anything he said . . . or I'll hurt you.

JULIA. Oh, Miss Lula.

LULA. Anyway, he didn't say nothin'. (HERMAN'S *mother enters the yard. She is a "poor white" about fifty-seven years old. She has risen above her poor farm background and tries to assume the airs of "quality." Her clothes are well-kept-shabby. She wears white shoes, a shirtwaist and skirt, drop earrings, a cameo brooch, a faded blue straw hat with a limp bit of veiling. She carries a heavy-black, oil-cloth bag. All in the yard give a step backward as she enters. She assumes an air of calm well-being. Almost as though visiting friends, but anxiety shows around the edges and underneath.* JULIA *approaches and* HERMAN'S MOTHER *abruptly turns to* MATTIE.)

HERMAN'S MOTHER. How do. (MATTIE, TEETA *and* PRINCESS *look at* HERMAN'S MOTHER. HERMAN'S MOTHER *is also curious about them.*)

MATTIE. (*In answer to a penetrating stare from the old woman.*) She's mine. I take care-a her. (*Speaking her defiance by ordering the children.*) Stay inside 'fore y'all catch the flu!

HERMAN'S MOTHER. (*To* LULA.) You were very kind to bring word . . . er . . .

LULA. Lula, Ma'am.

HERMAN'S MOTHER. The woman who nursed my second cousin's children . . . she had a name like that . . . Lu*lu* we called her.

LULA. My son, Nelson.

HERMAN'S MOTHER. Can see that. (MATTIE *and the*

children exit. FANNY *hurries in from the front entry. Is
most eager to establish herself on the good side of* HER-
MAN'S MOTHER. *With a slight bow. She is carrying the
silver tea service.)*

FANNY. Beg pardon, if I may be so bold, I'm Fanny,
the owner of all this property.

HERMAN'S MOTHER. (*Definitely approving of* FANNY.)
I'm . . . er . . . Miss Annabelle's mother.

FANNY. My humble pleasure . . . er . . . Miss er . . .

HERMAN'S MOTHER. (*After a brief, thoughtful pause.*)
Miss Thelma. (*They move aside but* FANNY *makes sure
others hear.*)

FANNY. Miss Thelma, this is not Squeeze-gut Alley.
We're just poor, humble, colored people . . . and everybody knows how to keep their mouth shut.

HERMAN'S MOTHER. I thank you.

FANNY. She wanted to get a doctor. I put my foot
down.

HERMAN'S MOTHER. You did right. (*Shaking her head,
confiding her troubles.*) Ohhhh, you don't know.

FANNY. (*With deep understanding.*) Ohhhh, yes, I do.
She moved in on me yesterday.

HERMAN'S MOTHER. Friend Fanny, help me to get
through this.

FANNY. I will. Now this is Julia, she's the one . . .
(HERMAN'S MOTHER *starts toward the house without
looking at* JULIA. FANNY *decides to let the matter drop.*)

HERMAN'S MOTHER. (*To* LULA.) Tell Uncle Greenlee
not to worry. He's holdin' the horse and buggy.

NELSON. (*Bars* LULA'S *way.*) Mama. I'll do it. (LULA
exits into her house. FANNY *leads her to the chair near*
HERMAN'S *bed.*)

ANNABELLE. Mama, if we don't call a doctor Herman's
gonna die.

HERMAN'S MOTHER. Everybody's gon' die. Just a
matter of when, where and how. A pretty silver service.

FANNY. English china. Belgian linen. Have a cup-a
tea?

HERMAN'S MOTHER. (*As a studied pronouncement.*) My son comes to deliver baked goods and the influenza strikes him down. Sickness, it's the war.

FANNY. (*Admiring her cleverness.*) Yes, Ma'am, I'm a witness. I saw him with the packages.

JULIA. Now please call the doctor.

ANNABELLE. Yes, please, Mama. No way for him to move 'less we pick him up bodily.

HERMAN'S MOTHER. Then we'll pick him up.

HERMAN. About Walter . . . your Walter . . . I'm sorry . . . (JULIA *tries to give* HERMAN *some water.*)

HERMAN'S MOTHER. Annabelle, help your brother. (ANNABELLE *gingerly takes glass from* JULIA.) Get that boy to help us. I'll give him a dollar. Now gather his things.

ANNABELLE. What things?

HERMAN'S MOTHER. His possessions, anything he owns, whatever is his. What you been doin' in here all this time? (FANNY *notices* JULIA *is about to speak, so she hurries her through the motions of going through dresser drawers and throwing articles into a pillow case.*)

FANNY. Come on, sugar, make haste.

JULIA. Don't go through my belongings. (*Tears through the drawers, flinging things around as she tries to find his articles.* FANNY *neatly piles them together.*)

FANNY. (*Taking inventory.*) Three shirts . . . one is kinda soiled.

HERMAN'S MOTHER. That's all right, I'll burn 'em.

FANNY. Some new undershirts.

HERMAN'S MOTHER. I'll burn them too.

JULIA. (*To* FANNY.) Put 'em down. I bought 'em and they're not for burnin'.

HERMAN'S MOTHER. (*Struggling to hold her anger in check.*) Fanny, go get that boy. I'll give him fifty cents.

FANNY. You said a dollar.

HERMAN'S MOTHER. All right, dollar it is. (FANNY *exits toward the front entry. In tense, hushed, excited tones, they argue back and forth.*) Now where's the billfold . . . there's papers . . . identity . . . (*Looks in* HERMAN's *coat pockets.*)

ANNABELLE. Don't make such-a to-do.

HERMAN'S MOTHER. You got any money of your own? Yes, I wanta know where's his money.

JULIA. I'm gettin' it.

HERMAN'S MOTHER. In her pocketbook. This is why the bakery can't make it.

HERMAN. I gave her the Gawd-damned money!

JULIA. And I know what Herman wants me to do . . .

HERMAN'S MOTHER. (*With a wry smile.*) I'm sure you know what he wants.

JULIA. I'm not gonna match words with you. Furthermore, I'm too much of a lady.

HERMAN'S MOTHER. A lady oughta learn how to keep her dress down.

ANNABELLE. Mama, you makin' a spectacle outta yourself.

HERMAN'S MOTHER. You a big simpleton. Men have nasty natures, they can't help it. A man would go with a snake if he only knew how. They cleaned out your wallet.

HERMAN. (*Shivering with a chill.*) I gave her the damn money. (JULIA *takes it from her purse.*)

HERMAN'S MOTHER. Where's your pocket-watch or did you give that too? Annabelle, get another lock put on that bakery door.

HERMAN. I gave her the money to go—to go to New York. (JULIA *drops the money in* HERMAN'S MOTHER'S *lap. She is silent for a moment.*)

HERMAN'S MOTHER. All right. Take it and go. It's never too late to undo a mistake. I'll add more to it. (*She puts the money on the dresser.*)

JULIA. I'm not goin' anywhere.

HERMAN'S MOTHER. Look here, girl, you leave him 'lone.

ANNABELLE. Oh, Mama, all he has to do is stay away.

HERMAN'S MOTHER. But he can't do it. Been years and he can't do it.

JULIA. I got him hoo-dooed, I sprinkle red pepper on his shirt-tail.

HERMAN'S MOTHER. I believe you.

HERMAN. I have a black woman . . . and I'm gon' marry her. I'm gon' marry her . . . got that? Pride needs a paper, for . . . for the sake of herself . . . that's dignity—tell me, what is dignity— Higher than the dirt it is . . . dignity is . . .

ANNABELLE. Let's take him to the doctor, Mama.

HERMAN'S MOTHER. When it's dark.

JULIA. Please!

HERMAN'S MOTHER. Nightfall. (JULIA *steps out on the porch but hears every word said in the room.*) I had such high hopes for him. (*As if* HERMAN *is dead.*) All my high hopes. When he wasn't but five years old I had to whip him so he'd study his John C. Calhoun speech. Oh, Calhoun knew 'bout niggers. He said, *"MEN* are not born . . . equal, or any other kinda way . . . MEN are *made"* . . . Yes, indeed, for recitin' that John C. Calhoun speech . . . Herman won first mention and a twenty dollar gold piece . . . at the Knights of The Gold Carnation picnic.

ANNABELLE. Papa changed his mind about the Klan. I'm glad.

HERMAN'S MOTHER. Yes, he was always changin' his mind about somethin'. But I was proud-a my men-folk that day. He spoke that speech . . . The officers shook my hand. They honored me . . . "That boy a-yours gonna be somebody." A poor baker-son layin' up with a nigger woman, a over-grown daughter in heat over a common sailor. I must be payin' for somethin' I did. Yesiree, do a wrong, God'll whip you.

ANNABELLE. I wish it was dark.

HERMAN'S MOTHER. I put up with a man breathin' stale whiskey in my face every night . . . pullin' and pawin' at me . . . always tired, inside and out . . . (*Deepest confidence she has ever shared.*) Gave birth to seven . . . five-a them babies couldn't draw breath.

ANNABELLE. (*Suddenly wanting to know more about her.*) Did you love Papa, Mama? Did you ever love him? . . .

HERMAN'S MOTHER. Don't ask me 'bout love . . . I don't know nothin' about it. Never mind love. This is my harvest . . .

HERMAN. Go home. I'm better. (HERMAN'S MOTHER's *strategy is to enlighten* HERMAN *and also wear him down. Out on the porch,* JULIA *can hear what is being said in the house.*)

HERMAN'S MOTHER. There's something wrong 'bout mis-matched things, be they shoes, socks, or people.

HERMAN. Go away, don't look at us.

HERMAN'S MOTHER. People don't like it. They're not gonna letcha do it in peace.

HERMAN. We'll go North.

HERMAN'S MOTHER. Not a thing will change except her last name.

HERMAN. She's not like others . . . she's not like that . . .

HERMAN'S MOTHER. All right, sell out to Schumann. I want my cash-money . . . You got no feelin' for me, I got none for you . . .

HERMAN. I feel . . . I feel what I feel . . . I don't know what I feel . . .

HERMAN'S MOTHER. Don't need to feel. Live by the law. Follow the law—law, law of the land. Obey the law!

ANNABELLE. We're not obeyin' the law. He should be quarantined right here. The city's tryin' to stop an epidemic.

HERMAN'S MOTHER. Let the city drop dead and you 'long with it. *Rather* be dead than disgraced. Your papa gimme the house and little money . . . I want my money back. (*She tries to drag* HERMAN *up in the bed.*) I ain't payin' for this. (*Shoves* ANNABELLE *aside.*) Let Schumann take over. A man who knows what he's doin'. Go with her . . . Take the last step against your own! Kill us all. Jesus, Gawd, save us or take us—

HERMAN. (*Screams.*) No! No! No! No!

HERMAN'S MOTHER. Thank Gawd, the truth is the light. Oh, Blessed Savior . . . (HERMAN *screams out, starting low and ever going higher. She tries to cover his mouth.* ANNABELLE *pulls her hand away.*) Thank you, Gawd, let the fire go out . . . this awful fire. (LULA *and* NELSON *enter the yard.*)

ANNABELLE. You chokin' him. Mama . . .

JULIA. (*From the porch.*) It's dark! It's dark. Now it's very dark.

HERMAN. One ticket on the Clyde Line . . . Julia . . . where are you? Keep singing . . . count . . . one, two . . . three. Over there, over there . . . send the word, send the word . . .

HERMAN'S MOTHER. Soon be home, son. (HERMAN *breaks away from the men, staggers to* MATTIE'S *porch and holds on.* MATTIE *smothers a scream and gets the children out of the way.* FANNY *enters.*)

HERMAN. Shut the door . . . don't go out . . . the enemy . . . the enemy . . . (*Recites the Calhoun speech.*) Men are not born infants are born! They grow to all the freedom of which the condition in which they were born permits. It is a great and dangerous error to suppose that all people are equally entitled to liberty.

JULIA. Go home— Please be still.

HERMAN. It is a reward to be earned, a reward reserved for the intelligent, the patriotic, the virtuous and deserving; and not a boon to be bestowed on a people too ignorant, degraded and vicious . . .

JULIA. You be still now, shut up.

HERMAN. . . . to be capable either of appreciating or of enjoying it.

JULIA. (*Covers her ears.*) Take him . . .

HERMAN. A black woman . . . not like the others . . .

JULIA. . . . outta my sight . . .

HERMAN. Julia, the ship is sinking . . . (HERMAN'S MOTHER *and* NELSON *help* HERMAN *up and out.*)

ANNABELLE. (*To* JULIA *on the porch.*) I'm sorry . . . so sorry it had to be this way. I can't leave with you thinkin' I uphold Herman, and blame you.

HERMAN'S MOTHER. (*Returning.*) You the biggest fool.

ANNABELLE. I say a man is responsible for his own behavior.

HERMAN'S MOTHER. And you, you oughta be locked up . . . workhouse . . . jail! Who you think you are!?

JULIA. I'm your damn daughter-in-law, you old bitch! The Battleship Bitch! The bitch who destroys with her filthy mouth. They could win the war with your killin' mouth. The son-killer, man-killer-bitch . . . She's killin' him 'cause he loved me more than anybody in the world. (FANNY *returns.*)

HERMAN'S MOTHER. Better off . . . He's better off dead in his coffin than live with the likes-a you . . . black thing! (*She is almost backing into* JULIA's *house.*)

JULIA. The black thing who bought a hot water bottle to put on your sick, white self when rheumatism threw you flat on your back . . . who bought flannel gowns to warm your pale, mean body. He never ran up and down King Street shoppin' for you . . . I bought what he took home to you . . .

HERMAN'S MOTHER. Lies . . . tear outcha lyin' tongue.

JULIA. . . . the lace curtains in your parlor . . . the shirt-waist you wearin'—I made them.

FANNY. Go *on* . . . I got her. (*Holds* JULIA.)

HERMAN'S MOTHER. Leave 'er go! The undertaker will have-ta unlock my hands off her black throat!

FANNY. Go on, Miss Thelma.

JULIA. Miss Thelma my ass! Her first name is Frieda. The Germans are here . . . in purple paint!

HERMAN'S MOTHER. Black, sassy nigger!

JULIA. Kraut, knuckle-eater, red-neck . . .

HERMAN'S MOTHER. Nigger whore . . . he used you for a garbage pail . . .

JULIA. White trash! Sharecropper! Let him die . . . let 'em all die . . . Kill him with your murderin' mouth —sharecropper bitch!

HERMAN'S MOTHER. Dirty black nigger . . .

JULIA. . . . If I wasn't black with all-a Carolina
'gainst me I'd be mistress of your house! (*To* ANNA-
BELLE.) Annabelle, you'd be married livin' in Brooklyn,
New York . . . (*To* HERMAN'S MOTHER.) . . . and I'd
be waitin' on Frieda . . . cookin' your meals . . .
waterin' that damn red-white and blue garden!

HERMAN'S MOTHER. Dirty black bitch.

JULIA. Daughter of a bitch!

ANNABELLE. Leave my mother alone! She's old . . .
and sick.

JULIA. But never sick enough to die . . . dirty ever-
lasting woman.

HERMAN'S MOTHER. (*Clinging to* ANNABELLE, *she
moves toward the front entry.*) I'm as high over you as
Mount Everest over the sea. White reigns supreme . . .
I'm white, you can't change that. (*They exit.* FANNY *goes
with them.*)

JULIA. Out! Out! Out! And take the last ten years-a
my life with you and . . . when he gets better . . . keep
him home. Killers, murderers . . . Kinsmen! Klansmen!
Keep him home. (*To* MATTIE.) Name and protection . . .
he can't gimme either one. (*To* LULA.) I'm gon' get down
on my knees and scrub where they walked . . . what
they touched . . . (*To* MATTIE.) . . . with brown soap
. . . hot lye-water . . . scaldin' hot . . . (*She dashes
into the house and collects an armful of bedding . . .*)
Clean! . . . Clean the whiteness outta my house . . .
clean everything . . . even the memory . . . no more
love . . . Free . . . free to hate-cha for the rest-a my
life. (*Back to the porch with her arms full.*) When I die
I'm gonna keep on hatin' . . . I dont' want any whiteness in my house. Stay out . . . out . . . (*Dumps the
things in the yard.*) . . . out . . . out . . . out . . .
and leave me to my black self!

BLACKOUT

ACT TWO

SCENE 2

TIME: *Early afternoon the following day.*

PLACE. *The same.*

In JULIA'S *room, some of the hope chest things are spilled out on the floor, bedspread, linens, silver cups. The half-emptied wine decanter is in a prominent spot. A table is set up in the yard. We hear the distant sound of a marching band. The excitement of a special day is in the air.* NELSON'S *army jacket hangs on his porch.* LULA *brings a pitcher of punch to table.* MATTIE *enters with* TEETA *and* PRINCESS; *she is annoyed and upset in contrast to* LULA'S *singing and gala mood. She scolds the children, smacks* TEETA'S *behind.*

MATTIE. They was teasin' the Chinaman down the street 'cause his hair is braided. (*To* CHILDREN.) If he ketches you, he'll cook you with onions and gravy.

LULA. (*Inspecting* NELSON'S *jacket.*) Sure will.

TEETA. Can we go play?

MATTIE. A mad dog might bite-cha.

PRINCESS. Can we go play?

MATTIE. No, you might step on a nail and get lock-jaw.

TEETA. Can we go play?

MATTIE. Oh, go on and play! I wish a gypsy would steal both of 'em! (JULIA *enters her room.*)

LULA. What's the matter, Mattie?

MATTIE. Them damn fool people at the Merchant Marine don't wanta give me my 'lotment money.

JULIA. (*Steps out on her porch with deliberate, defiant energy. She is wearing her wedding dress . . . carrying a wine glass. She is over-demonstrating a show of carefree abandon and joy.*) I'm so happy! I never been this happy in all my life! I'm happy to be alive, alive and livin for my people.

LULA. You better stop drinkin so much wine. (LULA *enters her house.*)

JULIA. But if you got no feelin's they can't be hurt!

MATTIE. Hey, Julia, the people at the Merchant Marine say I'm not married to October.

JULIA. Getcha license, honey, show your papers. Some of us, thang Gawd, got papers!

MATTIE. I don't have none.

JULIA. Why? Was October married before?

MATTIE. No, but I was. A good for nothin' named Delroy . . . I hate to call his name. Was years 'fore I met October. Delroy used to beat the hell outta me . . . tried to stomp me, grind me into the ground . . . callin' me such dirty names . . . Got so 'til I was shame to look at myself in a mirror. I was glad when he run off.

JULIA. Where'd he go?

MATTIE. I don't know. Man at the office kept sayin' . . . "You're not married to October" . . . and wavin' me 'way like that.

JULIA. Mattie, this state won't allow divorce.

MATTIE. Well, I never got one.

JULIA. You shoulda so you could marry October. You have to be married to get his benefits.

MATTIE. We was married. On Edisto Island. I had a white dress and flowers . . . everything but papers. We couldn't get papers. Elder Burns knew we was doin' best we could.

JULIA. You can't marry without papers.

MATTIE. What if your husband run off? And you got no money? Readin' from the Bible makes people married, not no piece-a paper. We're together eleven years, that oughta-a be legal.

JULIA. (*Puts down glass.*) No, it doesn't go that way.

MATTIE. October's out on the icy water, in the war-time, worryin' 'bout me 'n Teeta. I say he's my husband. Gotta pay Fanny, buy food. Julia, what must I do?

JULIA. I don't know.

MATTIE. What's the use-a so much-a education if you don't know what to do?

JULIA. You may's well just lived with October. Your marriage meant nothin'.

MATTIE. (*Standing angry.*) It meant somethin' to me if not to anybody else. It means I'm ice cream, too, strawberry. (MATTIE *heads for her house.*)

JULIA. Get mad with me if it'll make you feel better.

MATTIE. Julia, could you lend me two dollars?

JULIA. Yes, that's somethin' I can do besides drink this wine. (JULIA *goes into her room, to get the two dollars. Enter* FANNY, TEETA *and* PRINCESS.)

FANNY. Colored men don't know how to do nothin' right. I paid that big black boy cross the street . . . thirty cents to paint my sign . . . (*Sign reads . . .* GOODBYE COLORED BOYS . . . *on one side; the other reads . . .* FOR GOD AND CONTRY.) But he can't spell. I'm gon' call him a dumb darky and get my money back. Come on, children! (CHILDREN *follow laughing.*)

LULA. Why call him names!?

FANNY. 'Cause it makes him mad, that's why. (FANNY *exits with* TEETA *and* PRINCESS. JULIA *goes into her room. The* BELL MAN *enters carrying a display board filled with badges and flags . . . buttons, red and blue ribbons attached to the buttons . . . slogans . . .* THE WAR TO END ALL WARS. *He also carries a string of overseas caps [paper] and wears one. Blows a war tune on his tin flute.* LULA *exits.*)

BELL MAN. "War to end all wars . . ." Flags and badges! Getcha emblems! Hup-two-three . . . Flags and badges . . . hup-two-three! Hey, Aunty! Come back here! Where you at? (*Starts to follow* LULA *into her house.* NELSON *steps out on the porch and blocks his way.*)

NELSON. My mother is in her house. You ain't to come walkin' in. You knock.

BELL MAN. Don't letcha uniform go to your head, Boy, or you'll end your days swingin' from a tree.

LULA. (*Squeezing past* NELSON *dressed in skirt and open shirt-waist.*) Please, Mister, he ain't got good sense.

MATTIE. He crazy, Mister.

NELSON. Fact is, you stay out of here. Don't ever come back here no more.

BELL MAN. (*Backing up in surprise.*) He got no respect. One them crazies. I ain't never harmed a bareassed soul but, hot damn, I can got madder and badder than you. Let your uniform go to your head.

LULA. Yessir, he goin' back in the army today.

BELL MAN. Might not get there way he's actin.'

MATTIE. (*As* LULA *takes two one dollar bills from her bosom.*) He sorry right now, Mister, his head ain' right.

BELL MAN. (*Speaks to* LULA *but keeps an eye on* NELSON.) Why me? I try to give you a laugh but they say, "Play with a puppy and he'll lick your mouth." Familiarity makes for contempt.

LULA. (*Taking flags and badges.*) Yessir. Here's somethin' on my account . . . and I'm buyin' flags and badges for the children. Everybody know you a good man and do right.

BELL MAN. (*To* LULA.) You pay up by Monday. (*To* NELSON.) Boy, you done cut off your Mama's credit.

LULA. I don't blame you, Mister. (BELL MAN *exits.*)

NELSON. Mama, your new faith don't seem to do much for you.

LULA. (*Turning to him.*) Nelson, go on off to the war 'fore somebody kills you. I ain't goin' to let nobody spoil my day. (LULA *puts flags and badges on punchbowl table.* JULIA *comes out of her room, with the two dollars for* MATTIE—*hands it to her. Sound of Jenkins Colored Orphan Band is heard* [*Record: Ramblin' by Bunk Johnson*].)

JULIA. Listen, Lula . . . Listen, Mattie . . . it's Jenkin's Colored Orphan Band . . . Play! Play, you Orphan boys! Rise up higher than the dirt around you! Play! That's struttin' music, Lula!

LULA. It sure is! (LULA *struts, arms akimbo, head held high.* JULIA *joins her; they haughtily strut toward each other, then retreat with mock arrogance . . . exchange cold, hostile looks . . . A Carolina folk dance passed on from some dimly-remembered African beginning. Dance ends strutting.*)

JULIA. (*Concedes defeat in the dance.*) All right, Lula, strut me down! Strut me right on down! (*They end dance with breathless laughter and cross to* LULA's *porch.*)

LULA. Julia! Fasten me! Pin my hair.

JULIA. I'm not goin' to that silly parade, with the colored soldiers marchin' at the end of it. (LULA *sits on the stool.* JULIA *combs and arranges her hair.*)

LULA. Come on, we'll march behind the white folks whether they want us or not. Mister Herman's people got a nice house . . . lemon trees in the yard, lace curtains at the window.

JULIA. And red, white and blue flowers all around.

LULA. That Uncle Greenlee seems to be well-fixed.

JULIA. He works for the livery stable . . . cleans up behind horses . . . in a uniform.

LULA. That's nice.

JULIA. Weeds their gardens . . . clips white people's pet dogs . . .

LULA. Ain't that lovely? I wish Nelson was safe and nicely settled.

JULIA. Uncle Greenlee is a well-fed, tale-carryin' son-of-a-bitch . . . and that's the only kind-a love they want from us.

LULA. It's wrong to hate.

JULIA. They say it's wrong to love too.

LULA. We got to show 'em we're good, got to be three times as good, just to make it.

JULIA. Why? When they mistreat us who cares? We mistreat each other, who cares? Why we gotta be so good jus' for them?

LULA. Dern you, Julia Augustine, you hard-headed thing, 'cause they'll kill us if we not.

JULIA. They doin' it anyway. Last night I dreamed of the dead slaves—all the murdered black and bloody men silently gathered at the foot-a my bed. Oh, that awful silence. I wish the dead could scream and fight back. What they do to us . . . and all they want is to be loved in return. Nelson's not Greenlee. Nelson is a fighter.

LULA. (*Standing.*) I know. But I'm tryin' to keep him from findin' it out. (NELSON, *unseen by* LULA, *listens.*)

JULIA. Your hair looks pretty.

LULA. Thank you. A few years back I got down on my knees in the courthouse to keep him off-a the chain gang. I crawled and cried, "Please white folks, yall's everything, I'se nothin, yall's everything." the court laughed— I meant for 'em to laugh . . . then they let Nelson go.

JULIA. (*Pitying her.*) Oh, Miss Lula, a lady's not supposed to crawl and cry.

LULA. I was savin' his life. Is my skirt fastened? Today might be the last time I ever see Nelson. (NELSON *goes back in house.*) Tell him how life's gon' be better when he gets back. Make up what *should* be true. A man can't fight a war on nothin' . . . would you send a man off— to die on nothin'?

JULIA. That's sin, Miss Lula, leavin' on a lie.

LULA. That's all right—some truth has no nourishment in it. Let him feel good.

JULIA. I'll do my best. (MATTIE *enters carrying a colorful, expensive parasol. It is far beyond the price range of her outfit.*)

MATTIE. October bought it for my birthday 'cause he know I always wanted a fine-quality parasol. (FANNY *enters through the back entry,* CHILDREN *with her. The mistake on the sign has been corrected by pasting* OU *over the error.*)

FANNY. (*Admiring* MATTIE's *appearance.*) Just shows how the race can look when we wanta. I called Rusty Bennet a dumb darky and he wouldn't even get mad. Wouldn't gimme my money back either. A black Jew. (NELSON *enters wearing his Private's uniform with quartermaster insignia. He salutes them.*)

NELSON. Ladies. Was nice seein' you these few days. If I couldn't help, 'least I didn't do you no harm, so nothin' from nothin' leaves nothin'.

FANNY. (*Holds up her punch cup;* LULA *gives* JULIA *high sign.*) Get one-a them Germans for me. ·

JULIA. (*Stands on her porch.*) Soon, Nelson, in a little while . . . we'll have whatsoever our hearts desire. You're comin' back in glory . . . with honors and shining medals . . . And those medals and that uniform is gonna open doors for you . . . and for October . . . for all, all of the servicemen. Nelson, on account-a you we're gonna be able to go in the park. They're gonna take down the no-colored signs . . . and Rusty Bennet's gonna print new ones . . . Everybody welcome . . . Everybody welcome . . .

MATTIE. (*To* TEETA.) Hear that? We gon' go in the park.

FANNY. Some of us ain't ready for that.

PRINCESS. Me too?

MATTIE. You can go now . . . and me too if I got you by the hand.

PRINCESS. (*Feeling left out.*) Ohhhhh.

JULIA. We'll go to the band concerts, the museums . . . we'll go in the library and draw out books.

MATTIE. And we'll draw books.

FANNY. Who'll read 'em to you?

MATTIE. My Teeta!

JULIA. Your life'll be safe, you and October'll be heroes.

FANNY. (*Very moved.*) Colored heroes.

JULIA. And at last we'll come into our own. (ALL *cheer and applaud.* JULIA *steps down from porch.*)

NELSON. Julia, can you look me dead in the eye and say you believe all-a that?

JULIA. If you just gotta believe somethin', it may's well be that. (*Applause.*)

NELSON. (*Steps up on* JULIA'S *porch to make his speech.*) Friends, relatives and all other well-wishers. All-a my fine ladies and little ladies—all you good-lookin', tantalizin', pretty-eyed ladies—yeah, with your *kind* ways and your *mean* ways. I find myself a thorn among six lovely roses. Sweet little Teeta . . . the merry little Princess. Mattie, she so pretty 'til October better hurry up and come on back here. Fanny—uh—tryin' to help the race . . . a race woman. And Julia—my good friend. Mama—the only mama I got, I wanta thank you for savin' my life from time to time. What's hard ain't the goin', it's the comin' back. From the bottom-a my heart, I'd truly like to see y'all, each and every one-a you . . . able to go in the park and all that. I really would. So, with a full heart and a loaded mind, I bid you, as the French say, Adieu.

LULA. (*Bowing graciously, she takes* NELSON'S *arm and they exit.*) Our humble thanks . . . my humble pleasure . . . gratitude . . . thank you . . . (CHILDREN *wave their flags.*)

FANNY. (*To the* CHILDREN.) Let's mind our manners in front-a the downtown white people. Remember we're bein' judged.

PRINCESS. Me too?

MATTIE. (*Opening umbrella.*) Yes, you too.

FANNY. (*Leads the way and counts time.*) Step, step, one, two, step, step. (MATTIE, FANNY *and the* CHILDREN *exit.* HERMAN *enters yard by far gate, takes two long steamer tickets from his pocket.* JULIA *senses him, turns. He is carelessly dressed and sweating.*)

HERMAN. I bought our tickets. Boat tickets to New York.

JULIA. (*Looks at tickets.*) Colored tickets. You can't use yours. (*She lets tickets flutter to the ground.*)

HERMAN. They'll change and give one white ticket. You'll ride one deck, I'll ride the other . . .

JULIA. John C. Calhoun really said a mouthful—men are not born—men are made. Ten years ago—that's when you should-a bought tickets. You chained me to your mother for ten years.

HERMAN. (*Kneeling, picking up tickets.*) Could I walk out on 'em? . . . Ker-ist sake. I'm that kinda man like my father was . . . a debt-payer, a plain, workin' man—

JULIA. He was a member in good standin' of The Gold Carnation. What kinda robes and hoods did those plain men wear? For downin' me and mine. You won twenty dollars in gold.

HERMAN. I love you . . . I love work, to come home in the evenin' . . . to enjoy the breeze for Gawd's sake . . . But no, I never wanted to go to New York. The hell with Goddamn bread factories . . . I'm a stony-broke, half-dead, half-way gentleman . . . But I'm what I wanta be. A baker.

JULIA. You waited 'til you was half-dead to buy those tickets. I don't want to go either . . . Get off the boat, the same faces'll be there at the dock. It's that shop. It's that shop!

HERMAN. It's mine. I did want to keep it.

JULIA. Right . . . people pick what they want most.

HERMAN. (*Indicating the tickets.*) I did . . . you threw it in my face.

JULIA. Get out. Get your things and get out of my life. (*The remarks become counterpoint. Each rides through the other's speech.* HERMAN *goes in house.*) Must be fine to *own* somethin'—even if it's four walls and a sack-a flour.

HERMAN. (JULIA *has followed him into the house.*) My father labored in the street . . . liftin' and layin' down cobblestone . . . liftin' and layin' down stone 'til there was enough money to open a shop . . .

JULIA. My people . . . relatives, friends and strangers . . . they worked and slaved free for nothin' for some-a

the biggest name families down here . . . Elliots, Law-
rences, Ravenals . . . (HERMAN *is wearily gathering his
belongings.*)

HERMAN. Great honor, working for the biggest name
families. That's who you slaved for. Not me. The big
names.

JULIA. . . . the rich and the poor . . . we know you
. . . all of you . . . Who you are . . . where you came
from . . where you goin' . . .

HERMAN. What's my privilege . . . Good mornin',
good afternoon . . . pies are ten cents today . . . and
you can get 'em from Schumann for eight . . .

JULIA. "She's different" . . . I'm no different . . .

HERMAN. I'm white . . . did it give me favors and
friends?

JULIA. . . . "Not like the others" . . . We raised up
all-a these Carolina children . . . white and the black
. . . I'm just like all the rest of the colored women . . .
like Lula, Mattie . . . Yes, like Fanny!

HERMAN. Go here, go there . . . Philadelphia . . .
New York . . . Schumann wants me to go North too . . .

JULIA. We nursed you, fed you, buried your dead . . .
grinned in your face—cried 'bout your troubles—and
laughed 'bout ours.

HERMAN. Schumann . . . Alien robber . . . waitin'
to buy me out . . . My father . . .

JULIA. Pickin' up cobblestones . . . left him plenty-a
time to wear bed-sheets in that Gold Carnation Society . . .

HERMAN. He never hurt anybody.

JULIA. He hurts me. There's no room for you to love
him and me too . . . (*Sits.*) it can't be done—

HERMAN. The ignorance . . . he didn't know . . . the
ignorance . . . mama . . . they don't know.

JULIA. But *you* know. My father was somebody. He
helped put up Roper Hospital and Webster Rice Mills
after the earthquake wiped the face-a this Gawd-forsaken

city clean . . . a fine brick-mason he was . . . paid him one-third-a what they paid the white ones . . .

HERMAN. We were poor . . . No big name, no quality.

JULIA. Poor! My Gramma was a slave wash-woman bustin' suds for free! Can't get poorer than that.

HERMAN. (*Trying to shut out the sound of her voice.*) Not for me, she didn't!

JULIA. We the ones built the pretty white mansions . . . for free . . . the fishin' boats . . . for free . . . made your clothes, raised your food . . . for free . . . and I loved you—for free.

HERMAN. A Gawd-damn lie . . . nobody did for me . . . you know it . . . you know how hard I worked—

JULIA. If it's anybody's home down here it's mine . . . everything in the city is mine—why should I go anywhere . . . ground I'm standin' on—it's mine.

HERMAN. (*Sitting on foot of the bed.*) It's the ignorance . . . Lemme be, lemme rest . . . Ker-ist sake . . . It's the ignorance . . .

JULIA. After ten years you still won't look. All-a my people that's been killed . . . It's your people that killed 'em . . . all that's been in bondage—your people put 'em there—all that didn't go to school—your people kept 'em out.

HERMAN. But I didn't do it. Did I do it?

JULIA. They killed 'em . . . all the dead slaves . . . buried under a blanket-a this Carolina earth, even the cotton crop is nourished with hearts' blood . . . roots-a that cotton tangled and wrapped 'round my bones.

HERMAN. And you blamin' me for it . . .

JULIA. Yes! . . . For the one thing we never talk about . . . white folks killin' me and mine. You wouldn't let me speak.

HERMAN. I never stopped you . . .

JULIA. Every time I open my mouth 'bout what they do . . . you say . . . "Ker-ist, there it is again . . ." Whenever somebody was lynched . . . you 'n me would eat a very silent supper. It hurt me not to talk . . . what you don't say you swallow down . . . (*Pours wine.*)

HERMAN. I was just glad to close the door 'gainst what's out there. You did all the givin' . . . I failed you in every way.

JULIA. You nursed me when I was sick . . . paid my debts . . .

HERMAN. I didn't give my name.

JULIA. You couldn't . . . was the law . . .

HERMAN. I shoulda walked 'til we came to where it'd be all right.

JULIA. You never put any other woman before me.

HERMAN. Only, Mama, Annabelle, the customers, the law . . . the ignorance . . . I honored them while you waited and waited—

JULIA. You clothed me . . . you fed me . . . you were kind, loving . . .

HERMAN. I never did a damn thing for you. After ten years look at it—I never did a damn thing for you.

JULIA. Don't low-rate yourself . . . leave me something.

HERMAN. When my mother and sister came . . . I was ashamed. What am I doin' bein' ashamed of us?

JULIA. When you first came in this yard I almost died-a shame . . . so many times you was nothin' to me but white . . . times we were angry . . . damn white man . . . times I was tired . . . damn white man . . . but most times you were my husband, my friend, my lover . . .

HERMAN. Whatever is wrong, Julia . . . not the law . . . *me;* what I didn't do, with all-a my faults, spite-a all that . . . You gotta believe I love you . . . 'cause I do . . . That's the one thing I know . . . I love you . . . I love you.

JULIA. Ain't too many people in this world that get to be loved . . . really loved.

HERMAN. We gon' take that boat trip . . . You'll see, you'll never be sorry.

JULIA. To hell with sorry. Let's be glad!

HERMAN. Sweetheart, leave the ignorance outside . . . (*Stretches out across the bed.*) Don't let that doctor in here . . . to stand over me shakin' his head.

JULIA. (*Pours water in a silver cup.*) Bet you never drank from a silver cup. Carolina water is sweet water . . . Wherever you go you gotta come back for a drink-a this water. Sweet water, like the breeze that blows 'cross the battery.

HERMAN. (*Happily weary.*) I'm gettin' old, that ain' no joke.

JULIA. No, you're not. Herman, my real weddin' cake . . . I wanta big one . . .

HERMAN. Gonna bake it in a wash-tub . . .

JULIA. We'll put pieces of it in little boxes for folks to take home and dream on.

HERMAN. . . . But let's don't give none to your landlady . . . Gon' get old and funny-lookin' like Robbie m'boy and . . . and . . .

JULIA. And Mable . . .

HERMAN. (*Breathing heavier.*) Robbie says "Mable, where's my keys" . . . Mable— Robbie— Mable— (*Lights change, shadows grow longer.* MATTIE *enters the yard.*)

MATTIE. Hey, Julia! (*Sound of carriage wheels in front of the main house.* MATTIE *enters* JULIA'S *house. As she sees* HERMAN.) They 'round there, they come to get him, Julia. (JULIA *takes the wedding band and chain from around her neck, gives it to* MATTIE *with tickets.*)

JULIA. Surprise. Present.

MATTIE. For me?

JULIA. Northern tickets . . . and a wedding band.

MATTIE. I can't take that for nothing.

JULIA. You and Teeta are my people.

MATTIE. Yes.

JULIA. You and Teeta are my family. Be my family.

MATTIE. We your people whether we blood kin or not. (MATTIE *exits to her own porch.*)

FANNY. (*Offstage.*) No . . . No, Ma'am. (*Enters with* LULA. LULA *is carrying the wilted bouquet.*) Julia! They think Mr. Herman's come back. (HERMAN'S MOTHER *enters with* ANNABELLE. *The old lady is weary and subdued.* ANNABELLE *is almost without feeling.* JULIA *is on her porch waiting.*)

JULIA. Yes, Fanny, he's here. (LULA *retires to her doorway.* JULIA *silently stares at them, studying each* WOMAN, *seeing them with new eyes. She is going through that rising process wherein she must reject them as the molders and dictators of her life.*) Nobody comes in my house.

FANNY. What kind-a way is that?

JULIA. Nobody comes in my house.

ANNABELLE. We'll quietly take him home.

JULIA. You can't come in.

HERMAN'S MOTHER. (*Low-keyed, polite and humble simplicity.*) You see my condition. Gawd's punishin' me . . . Whippin' me for somethin' I did or didn't do. I can't understand this . . . I prayed, but ain't no understandin' Herman's dyin'. He's almost gone. It's right and proper that he should die at home in his own bed. I'm askin' humbly . . . or else I'm forced to get help from the police.

ANNABELLE. Give her a chance . . . She'll do right . . . won'tcha? (HERMAN *stirs. His breathing becomes harsh and deepens into the sound known as the "death rattle."* MATTIE *leads the* CHILDREN *away.*)

JULIA. (*Not unkindly.*) Do whatever you have to do. Win the war. Represent the race. Call the police. (*She enters her house, closes the door and bolts it.* HERMAN'S MOTHER *leaves through the front entry.* FANNY *slowly follows her.*) I'm here, do you hear me? (*He tries to answer but can't.*) We're standin' on the deck-a that Clyde Line Boat . . . wavin' to the people on the shore . . . Your mama, Annabelle, my Aunt Cora . . . all of our friends . . . the children . . . all wavin' . . . "Don't stay 'way too long . . . Be sure and come back . . .

We gon' miss you . . . Come back, we need you" . . .
But we're goin' . . . The whistle's blowin', flags wavin'
. . . We're takin' off, ridin' the waves so smooth and easy
. . . There now . . . (ANNABELLE *moves closer to the
house as she listens to* JULIA.) . . . the bakery's fine
. . . all the orders are ready . . . out to sea . . . on our
way . . . (*The weight has lifted, she is radiantly happy.
She helps him gasp out each remaining breath. With each
gasp he seems to draw a step nearer to a wonderful goal.*)
Yes . . . Yes . . . Yes . . . Yes . . . Yes . . . Yes . . .

CURTAIN

PROPERTY PLOT

PRESET—*Onstage* U. C. *House:*

On bureau top:
Ceramic box with coins
Dresser tray with bottles
Hairbrush
Comb
Hand mirror
Lamp

n large bureau drawer:
Man's sweater
2 men's shirts
Assorted men's underwear
Pillow case

On bed table top:
Lamp
Wine decanter with wine
2 wine glasses
Clock
Writing paper and pencils—bed table drawer
Broom—S. R. of bed table

On side table:
2 goblets
Condiments carrier
candelabra

On D. S. R. *table top:*
Tea cup and saucer
Scissors
Hanger
Shirtwaist
Spool of thread
Coin purse with 2 dollars—D.S.R. table drawer

In hope chest:
Quilt
Wedding dress
Peel (wrapped)
Pastry bag (wrapped)

67

On bed:
2 pillows with cases
2 sheets
Bed spread
Satchel—s. r. of d. s. l. chest

In satchel:
Trousers
Men's shirt
Shaving mug
Shaving brush
Shaving strap
Picture of "Aunt Cora"

Upstage of u. c. *House:*
Rug
Water pitcher with water
2 silver cups
Water glass
Medicine tray
   With medicine bottles
   Bowl with wet rag
   Paregoric bottle
   Glass of paregoric
Spoon
2 hand towels
Hot water bottle
Wine glass
Tea kettle with water
2 pillows with cases

Onstage Yard—s.l. *porch:*
Pump on housing—d. s. c. (Pump must be practical)

On housing:
Soap dish and soap
Tin cup
Wooden bench—d. s. r.
Stump—u. s. c. in front of s. c. house
Axe—in stump
Wooden bucket—in front of s. l. porch
Brick fireplace—cooking area—u. s. r.
Cooking pot—on bricks

s. l. of stove area:
  Paper twists and sticks
  Box matches

Against u. s. r. fence set dressing:
  Barrel
  Wash tub
  Wash boards
Clothes line—between c. house and s. l. porch

On clothes line:
  Clothes pin bag and pins
  Khaki shirt
2 stools—on s. l. porch
Tray—on stool
Ironing board—on s. l. porch
  On ironing board:
  Iron
    Clothes brush
    Army jacket (costume)

Stage Left—Table:
  LULA:
    Slop jar
    Coffee pot with coffee
    Laundry basket with laundry—laundry is wet
    Flower basket with finished flowers, scissors
    Funeral wreath
    Altar with Bible
    Hanky with 2 dollars

  NELSON:
    Cup and saucer
    Shaving mug with shaving brush
    Shoe brush
    Clothes brush (from onstage)
    Wooden bucket (from onstage)

  BELL MAN:
    Suitcase with wares
      Sheet
      Stockings
    "Sample"
    Hand bell

TEETA:
  Milk pail
  Cookie
  Biscuit

HERMAN:
  Cake with 10 candles
  Cake box with ribbon
  Bag with biscuits
  Box matches
  Ring box with ring on chain
  Wallet with $17.00

NELSON:
  Flowers in florist paper

FANNY:
  "OU" paste on—for sign
  Punch table with punch bowl and punch
  6 punch cups
  Ladle
  Decorations for porch—S. L.

HERMAN:
  2 steamer tickets
  Sign "We are American Citizens"

Stage Right—Table:
  MATTIE:
    Switch
    Candy tray with removable candy
      Wooden bowl—with molasses
      Wooden spoon
    Gourd rattle

  FANNY:
    Letter with $10.00 in envelope—no stamp
    Police whistle on chain
    Silver tray with tea service
      Spoon
      Cloth napkin
      Cup and saucer
    Sign on stick
      "Goodbye Colored Boys" (one side)
      For God and Contry (other side)

TEETA:
  Rag doll

PRINCESS:
  Jump rope
  Bean bag

BELL MAN:
  Display board
  with 2 flags, 2 badges
  Paper hat
  Bell (from S. L. preset)

SHOW:
  Strike iron board and iron from S. L. porch

Between Act One and Act Two—Intermission.

STRIKE:
  From S. C. house:
  Wedding dress
  Sweater
  Peel
  Wine decanter
  Wine glasses
  Cake and cake box and sign
  Shirt waist
  Hanger
  From yard area:
  Altar
  Clothes pin bag
  Laundry basket
  Chamber pot
  Axe
  Flower basket
  Wooden bowl and spoon
  Tea cups and saucer

ADD:
  To D. S. R. table:
  2 hand towels
  Medicine tray
  Hot water bottle
  Scissors

Side table:
    Water pitcher
    Water glass
To hope chest:
    Trivet
To bed:
    2 pillows

Between Act Two and Act Three—Intermission.

STRIKE:
  From house:
    Water glass
    Trivet
    Medicine tray
    Scissors
    Hand towels
    Coin purse
    Hot water bottle
  From yard:
    Bedding

ADD:
  To bed table:
    2 silver cups
    Water pitcher
  To D. S. R. *table:*
    Wine decanter
    Wine glass

REMAKE BED
  D. S. L.:
    Punch table
      With punch bowl
      6 cups
Decorations—to S. L. porch

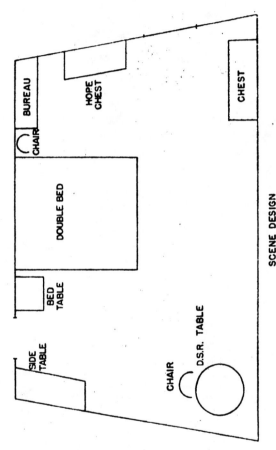

SCENE DESIGN
"WEDDING BAND"

OTHER TITLES AVAILABLE FROM SAMUEL FRENCH

THE RIVERS AND RAVINES
Heather McDonald

Drama / 9m, 5f / Unit Set

Originally produced to acclaim by Washington D.C.'s famed Arena Stage. This is an engrossing political drama about the contemporary farm crisis in America and its effect on rural communities.

"A haunting and emotionally draining play. A community of farmers and ranchers in a small Colorado town disintegrates under the weight of failure and thwarted ambitions. Most of the farmers, their spouses, children, clergyman, banker and greasy spoon proprietress survive, but it is survival without triumph. This is an *Our Town* for the 80's."
– *The Washington Post*

OTHER TITLES AVAILABLE FROM SAMUEL FRENCH

OUTRAGE
Itamar Moses

Drama / 8m, 2f / Unit Set

In Ancient Greece, Socrates is accused of corrupting the young with his practice of questioning commonly held beliefs. In Renaissance Italy, a simple miller named Menocchio runs afoul of the Inquisition when he develops his own theory of the cosmos. In Nazi Germany, the playwright Bertolt Brecht is persecuted for work that challenges authority. And in present day New England, a graduate student finds himself in the center of a power struggle over the future of the University. An irreverent epic that spans thousands of years, *Outrage* explores the power of martyrdom, the power of theatre, and how the revolutionary of one era become the tyrant of the next.

THREE YEARS FROM "THIRTY"
Mike O'Malley

Dramatic Comedy / 4m, 3f / Unit set

This funny, poignant story of a group of 27-year-olds who have known each other since college sold out during its limited run at New York City's Sanford Meisner Theater. Jessica Titus, a frustrated actress living in Boston, has become distraught over local job opportunities and she is feeling trapped in her long standing relationship with her boyfriend Tom. She suddenly decides to pursue her dreams in New York City. Unbeknownst to her, Tom plans to propose on the evening she has chosen to leave him. The ensuing conflict ripples through their lives and the lives of their roommates and friends, leaving all of them to reconsider their careers, the paths of their souls and the questions, demands and definition of commitment.

OTHER TITLES AVAILABLE FROM SAMUEL FRENCH

MURDER AT CAFÉ NOIR
David Landau
Music and Lyrics by Nikki Stern

Mystery / 4m, 3f / Interior

The most popular mystery dinner show in the country, *Murder at Café Noir* has enjoyed weekly productions coast to coast since its premiere in 1989. This forties detective story come to life features Rick Archer, P.I., out to find a curvaceous runaway on the forgotten island of Mustique, a place stuck in a black and white era. The owner of the Café Noir has washed ashore, murdered, and Rick's quarry was the last person seen with him. He employs his hard boiled talents to find the killer. Was it the French madame and club manager, the voodoo priestess, the shyster British attorney, the black marketeer or the femme fatale? The audience votes twice on what they want Rick to do next and these decisions change the flow of this comic tribute to the Bogart era.

"Fast and funny satire."
– *Los Angeles Times*

This whodunit is darn good it's the kind of show that lingers on you mind, like a dame's perfume
– *Maryland Journal*

SAMUEL FRENCH STAFF

Nate Collins
President

Ken Dingledine
Director of Operations,
Vice President

Bruce Lazarus
Executive Director

Rita Maté
Director of Finance

ACCOUNTING

Lori Thimsen | Director of Licensing Compliance
Nehal Kumar | Senior Accounting Associate
Josephine Messina | Accounts Payable
Helena Mezzina | Royalty Administration
Joe Garner | Royalty Administration
Jessica Zheng | Accounts Receivable
Andy Lian | Accounts Receivable
Zoe Qiu | Accounts Receivable
Charlie Sou | Accounting Associate
Joann Mannello | Orders Administrator

BUSINESS AFFAIRS

Lysna Marzani | Director of Business Affairs
Kathryn McCumber | Business Administrator

CUSTOMER SERVICE AND LICENSING

Brad Lohrenz | Director of Licensing Development
Billie Davis | Licensing Service Manager
Fred Schnitzer | Business Development Manager
Melody Fernandez | Amateur Licensing Supervisor
Laura Lindson | Professional Licensing Supervisor
John Tracey | Professional Licensing Associate
Kim Rogers | Amateur Licensing Associate
Matthew Akers | Amateur Licensing Associate
Jay Clark | Amateur Licensing Associate
Alicia Grey | Amateur Licensing Associate
Ashley Byrne | Amateur Licensing Associate
Jake Glickman | Amateur Licensing Associate
Chris Lonstrup | Amateur Licensing Associate
Jabez Zuniga | Amateur Licensing Associate
Glenn Halcomb | Amateur Licensing Associate
Derek Hassler | Amateur Licensing Associate
Jennifer Carter | Amateur Licensing Associate

EDITORIAL AND PUBLICATIONS

Amy Rose Marsh | Literary Manager
Ben Coleman | Editorial Associate
Gene Sweeney | Graphic Designer
David Geer | Publications Supervisor
Charlyn Brea | Publications Associate
Tyler Mullen | Publications Associate

MARKETING

Abbie Van Nostrand | Director of Marketing
Alison Sundstrom | Marketing Associate

OPERATIONS

Joe Ferreira | Product Development Manager
Casey McLain | Operations Supervisor
Danielle Heckman | Office Coordinator, Reception

SAMUEL FRENCH BOOKSHOP (LOS ANGELES)

Joyce Mehess | Bookstore Manager
Cory DeLair | Bookstore Buyer
Jennifer Palumbo | Customer Service Associate
Sonya Wallace | Bookstore Associate
Tim Coultas | Bookstore Associate
Monté Patterson | Bookstore Associate
Robin Hushbeck | Bookstore Associate
Alfred Contreras | Shipping & Receiving

LONDON OFFICE

Felicity Barks | Submissions Associate
Steve Blacker | Bookshop Associate
David Bray | Customer Services Associate
Zena Choi | Professional Licensing Associate
Robert Cooke | Assistant Buyer
Stephanie Dawson | Amateur Licensing Associate
Simon Ellison | Retail Sales Manager
Jason Felix | Royalty Administration
Susan Griffiths | Amateur Licensing Associate
Robert Hamilton | Amateur Licensing Associate
Lucy Hume | Publications Associate
Nasir Khan | Management Accountant
Simon Magniti | Royalty Administration
Louise Mappley | Amateur Licensing Associate
James Nicolau | Despatch Associate
Martin Phillips | Librarian
Zubayed Rahman | Despatch Associate
Steve sanderson | Royalty Administration Supervisor
Roger Sheppard | I.T. Manager
Geoffrey Skinner | Company Accountant
Peter Smith | Amateur Licensing Associate
Garry Spratley | Customer Service Manager
David Webster | UK Operations Director